Rece,

THE ART OF
COLLABORATION

I have loved getting to know you over the summer — you are a wonderful young woman and will do great things! Don't lose your passions — they are what make you, you!

Sydney ♡

THE ART OF COLLABORATION

SYDNEY ELIZABETH WELCH

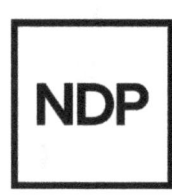

NEW DEGREE PRESS

THE ART OF COLLABORATION

ISBN

978-1-63676-634-8 *Paperback*

978-1-63676-229-6 *Kindle Ebook*

978-1-63676-232-6 *Digital Ebook*

My grandfather has often said to me, "At the end of your life you're lucky if you can count the true friends you've had on one hand."

I know who some of you are, and I am excited to find out about the rest of you. While I can't predict what that handful will look like for me in sixty-two years, I would like to dedicate this book to my handful.

CONTENTS

ACKNOWLEDGMENTS

———

Deciding to write a book in January was an exciting decision. I never could have anticipated how many incredible people had to come together to get my book published. I really believe in the value of working together, and I have so many people to thank for working together with me on this book.

I am so grateful for each and every one of you and our collaboration.

To Ellie: there was a point when I was thinking about not finishing this book, and your love and support was exactly what I needed to get it done. Thank you for filling my cup again and again.

To all the people who have asked me about the book, supported me, said you would read it, or asked for my signature: you are all so important to me; there are not enough pages to express the gratitude I have for every single one of you. To all of the educators I have had since I was in pre-school who have encouraged my creativity, especially Amy Brown, Kevin Calisto, Allie Micheletti, Christopher Cerski, and Jill

Pederson: I have always been a little eccentric, but having adults foster and support my creativity is what kept it from going away. Thank you.

Thank you to all of my family members: my parents, whose love and support I am only beginning to understand; my brother, for always being honest (even when I don't want him to be). My Aunt Re, for always being there *no matter what.* Thank you to the Geib Treib for your humor and friendship. There are some people who are not here anymore who I know would be part of this journey if they were, but they are with me in spirit.

Thank you to Eric Koester for finding me and convincing me that I had what it takes to write a book! Thank you to Brian Bies and the entire New Degree Press team. You have made the process so much easier than I imagine it would have been any other way. I owe some of the deepest gratitude to my editors, Cortni Meritt and Kristin Gustafson, for never saying no to my eccentric ideas and being so flexible with my crazy schedule. Thank you to Portsmouth Abbey School and all of my English teachers for teaching me how to write and always holding me to high standards. Thank you to Judge Cerski and Jill Pederson for refining my writing skills and demanding my best from me. I have to include David Guinn, who recognized my capabilities and encouraged me to step into them. Having mentors and teachers who accepted nothing but my best made me expect it from myself.

And thank you to everyone who contributed their time and talents during my interview process, pre-ordered the book, helped spread the word about *The Art of Collaboration* to gather amazing momentum, and helped me publish this book that I am so proud of. I am sincerely grateful for every single one of you:

Mark Harrison	Jill Pederson
Julia Richards	Peggy Ciarciello
Abigail Ryan	Christy Meltzer
Keith Bacote	Thomas Flaherty
Connor Johnson	Nora Phinn
Suzanne Farley	Joann Genduso
Kelsea Funk	Barbara Swoyer
Mary Shipman	Jeremy Sabathne
Ian Schreiber	Travis Lukens
William Cook	Lorraine Benner
Tom Shields	Laurence Maschio
Kathleen Leone	Sky Coleman
Joe Michaud	Caitlin Mcnesby
Danielle Hurd	Ibtissam Jait
Kevin Mason	Maddy Devita
Shae Coniglio	Jenifer Myers
Liam Modesti	Anthony Dunn
Courtney Hurd	Mackenzie Grahek
Isabella Martinez	Christopher Cerski
Jennifer Plousis	Adam Simone

Dana Martino	Shade Foreman
Rot Sarah	Kronborg
William Mack	Scott Winter
Jules Johnston	Ann Connolly
Jody Mooney	Cece Carton
Kyle Henofer	Beth O'Neill
Matt D'Arrigo	Daniel Bower
Cody Allen	Kara McDermott
Logan Harrigan	Eric Koester
Kevin Batchelor	Jen Moses
Katherine Tortorella	Marco Guiterrez
Jennifer Yates	Jeremy Gosbee
Bernard Dunlevy	Keith Vickery
Gregory Melang	Judy Quigley
Bobby Shallcross	Susanna Smith
Claudia Jones	Tammy Balthaser Weaver
Meghan Tome	Ed Mackin Sr.
Carly Johnston	Grace Benzal
Chris Andreychik	Gabriella Meridionale
Samantha Tulli	Susan Wright
Brian Siket	Zaid Albukhari
Jeremy Deedes	Betsy Stefferud
Leo Voloshin	Leaugeay Genduso

Collin Reynolds

Leslie Wohlbruck

Margaret Burke

Danny Nunan

Ally Lugas

Naomi Barbary-Burke

Ellie Kestner

Nicole Loffredo

Stephanie McNesby

Libby Mohn

Liz Moffie

Catherine Kelly

George Achhamer

Thomas Geib Jr.

Mikaila Milks

Carita Geib

Theresa Geib

Alice Marie Geib

Sarah Dashew

Ryan Conner

David Guinn

George Humphreys

Joseph Macomber

Bobby Cloughen

Connor Geiman

William McKay

Kathleen Moyer

Thomas Mahar

Garrett Nelson

Connor Reardon

Michelle Spatz

Peter Reis

Mary Millar

Emily Mackin

Jillian Salerno

Alexa Nepa

Samantha Froman

Paul Nussbaum

Josh Okoro

Cathy Shields

Farris Fakhoury

Lea Mirabile

Molly Foster

Grace Cavanagh

Leslie Dashew

Morgan Moppert

Jess McGlynn

Pamela O'neill

Kayla Nilsen

Emma Beveridge

Sheri Hachey

Flyville

Javier Fernandez

Noel Garapola

Kristy Leone

Karli Pfleghaar

Jodi Butters

Michael Hartman

Phil Eastabrook

Alexander Deedes

Melissa Kestner

Tim Kernan

Gabriella Audi

Collin Marino

Amy Hoover

Carly Roeck

Carlyn Nordeman

Alice Froman

Morgan Perry

Kyle Schachner

Ted and Doris Fergus

Gabrielle Moyer

Finn O'Farrel

Nick Armero

Will Custis

Nicholas D'Souza

Patrick MacDonald

Daisy Steinthat

Andrea Genduso

Ryan Conroy

Kris Schaible

Tricia Goodman

Hannah Weissberger

John Power

Zach Troast

Kim Barder

Will Welch

Peter Vergara

Erin Perry

Kristin McSorley

Kalle White

Christina Flatley

Morgan Myers

Julia Lindsay

Veandra Selby

Bernadette Geib

Jena Lasewicz

Addison Wright

Spencer Marchel

George McCathy

Dan Sucharski

Jeannie and Bill Welch

Allie Micheletti

Catherine Francheski

Sara Bertuccio

Claire Froman

Sallie Callahan

Sarah Long

John George

Annabel Brown

Andrea Sharp

Diana Williams

Gerald Williams

George MacDonald

Matthew Mayo

Daniel Nordeman

Caitlin McMorrow

Mckenna Coffey

Paulina Power

Jamie Brandenburger

Mandy Strangis

Brooke Maden

Emily Froman

JT Flatley

Luke Coffey

Dana Giannuario

Chris Williamson

INTRODUCTION

———

In the summer of 2018, I became grossly aware of the major issues regarding climate change and plastic pollution. The activist within me immediately wanted to make changes everywhere I could. Living in a beach town, I was inspired to approach local restaurants and businesses to try and pitch to them why they needed to eliminate plastic and become all-around more sustainable. I was met with great criticism, not only from these business owners, but also from friends and family. Many suggested that at nineteen, I did not have the authority to go into businesses and tell them how they ought to be running. I put the project on hold and decided to generate some more research and a more polished platform, and in summer 2019, I reached out again.

Only one business agreed to meet with me and ultimately heard me out, but it didn't run with my ideas. After two summers of failures, I realized my major problem: I was doing it all alone. I didn't have anyone to bounce my ideas off of; I was a one-man show trying to change the world. It occurred to me that what I needed to do was find like-minded people and gather them in a space that fit our innovation and desire to create a new normal.

I studied abroad for the whole of my junior year, and I met so many interesting characters. My first semester in Barcelona, Spain, is where the inspiration for the space I wanted to create came from. During my second semester in Florence, Italy, I realized that even though I wasn't finding people at home who had my same visions, they were out there, and I had finally met some of them. My ideas were no longer met with criticism and "You can't do that," but rather, "What does that look like?" and, "Here's an idea to make it even better." All of a sudden, I regained the momentum to take on this initiative and began branding myself and mapping out my vision. This book is one of the first concrete steps in obtaining that vision—an analysis and case-by-case study on the value of collaboration and how it is necessary for creative success. As more people and places inspired me, my goals shifted, and while sustainability is still a major value in my life, I decided to push my vision even further.

I wanted to write this story to help me gain the authority to discuss the power of collaboration and really pinpoint what it is that makes collaboration the key to success. We hear things all the time like "teamwork makes the dream work," "safety in numbers," "there's no 'I' in 'team,'" and "many hands make light work." I think if we trace the art world back to the Renaissance, when most work was emerging from workshops with pupils and apprentices, to now, authorship and creative work has become more singular and less valuable if it is collaborative. I want to change this narrative and encourage collaboration and the importance of using everyone's strengths to make something truly wonderful.

Another motivation is to really identify why collaboration is viewed in a negative light sometimes and to try to trace the historical roots of collaboration, when they disappeared, and why. Leonardo da Vinci, arguably one of the most famous people to ever live and one of the most famous artists known to man, was a collaborator. He began his training as an artist in a sculpture studio! He had apprentices, students, and followers, and in those times, it wasn't unusual to see many hands on one work.[1] Why has the concept of authorship changed, and can we shift our ideas about authorship back and embrace a workshop style of creation again? The Renaissance produced some of the most important and enlightened works, ideas, and inventions in the world, many of which are still in play today, and if we can see how those collaborative efforts really contributed to success before FaceTime, email, and Google Drive were available, we can certainly find a reason to argue that the best way to succeed is through collaboration. In the big world of ideas, nothing is really unique or new: we just have to find a new way to explore something that already exists.

I have this big-picture idea for a space where young innovators and creative types can come to hang out, bounce ideas off of each other, and then eventually get exposure and access to the types of people who can make their work and ideas take off. This "space" all starts with this book and really uncovering why collaboration is necessary and what sort of things happen when it is used, embraced, and understood. No one is perfect, and in order to achieve the best results, I really want to see and foster an environment where people can work together and find a way to achieve success—in a way that is not dissimilar from the process I am currently undergoing to write this book!

---

1   Sydney Welch, "An Analysis of the Attribution of the Louvre Abu Dhabi Salvator Mundi." (Undergraduate thesis, Arcadia University, 2020).

This idea is big, however, and requires a lot of moving parts and a lot of support and funding. In order to really get investors to back me and this plan, I need to have some authority on the art of collaboration. By interviewing successful artists, authors, musicians, and CEOs, I can slowly start to identify what is required to make a collaborative effort come to fruition and really succeed, and thus investors will be open to handing their money to a twenty-two-year-old. My hope is that by the end of this book, I will have a platform to advocate not only for my own authority on this topic, but for the necessity of my "space" and a convincing argument for investors to support me. I really believe in the power of collaboration and its ability to transform our ideas.

There is an inherent need for human connection in our society right now. This is fundamental to the nature of humans, and this need has been exacerbated due to the COVID-19 pandemic and the increased amount of people who have been staying at home and sheltering in place. Humans are social creatures and are ultimately suffering without their daily routines that foster this connection; we now recognize how important human connection is to our well-being and success, not only in our careers, but in our personal lives as well. We can stay in our homes and have everything we need... with the use of grocery delivery, Amazon Prime, and Wi-Fi, we have come to lose the human interaction that occurs in markets, grocery stores, and in-person meetings. My hope is that whether you're reading this book with professional or personal aspirations, you will see that collaboration will help to strengthen your relationships.

Collaboration is not a *new* idea: it has deep roots in our human history and the history of society. There was a time, not so long ago, when communities depended on each person to uphold their roles: butchers, seamstresses, bakers, mechanics, florists, and milkmen. Now, all of those roles have been compressed into services like supermarkets or virtual marketplaces. This desire for convenience has stripped us of the easiest ways to foster human interaction in our everyday lives and has subsequently made stay-at-home orders actually feasible. The lack of human interaction led one-third of Americans to suffer from COVID-19-related increased anxiety and depression, according to Hartford Healthcare.[2] I believe these mental health issues could be eased by collaborating and increasing human connection—even if not physical.

Part One of the book is going to give us a rundown of collaboration. What is it? Where does it come from? How does it work? We're going to look at the golden age of human creativity, the Italian Renaissance, and analyze how collaboration was at play and what happened to it. We will dive into an example of the modern workshop and hear from an apprentice emerging from an age-old tradition. We will look at the science, the data points, and the psychology behind collaboration to better understand what it is we're talking about. Then you will hear about me and see why I've decided to write this book during the COVID-19 pandemic and what collaboration has done for me personally.

---

2 "These Age Groups Most Affected by COVID-Related Depression, Anxiety," Hartford HealthCare. https://hartfordhealthcare.org/about-us/news-press/news-detail?articleid=26831.

PART ONE

AN IN-DEPTH LOOK AT COLLABORATION

THE *SALVATOR MUNDI*

On the evening of November 15, 2017, I sat in Glenside, Pennsylvania, with Jill Pederson during a Cheltenham Township meeting, waiting to be recognized for my work on the Arcadia Public Art Project. It was such an honor to be recognized by the township for my collaborative work with David Guinn and my fellow student apprentices. To me, this date was significant not only because of this service award, but because on the same night, at the same time, The *Salvator Mundi* painting by Leonardo da Vinci was up for auction at Christie's Auction House. Instead of focusing on the meeting, my professor and I were anxiously checking our phones (discreetly) as the price of the painting kept rising. One million turned into two million, which went to three million. We were aghast. We weren't the only ones: if you watch the video of the auction, you see the attendees in complete dismay.

The phone at Christie's continued to ring, the number continued to rise, and our heart rates continued to increase. On the evening of November 15, 2017, The *Salvator Mundi* sold at Christie's Auction House for 450 million dollars as an autograph Leonardo da Vinci painting. This record-breaking price tag was undoubtedly due to the authorship of the painting accredited to Leonardo, and it became the most expensive painting ever sold. In the years since the sale, scholarship has been released speculating about the authenticity of the authorship and attribution.

Leonardo himself worked on projects that are attributed to his teacher Andrea del Verrocchio.[1] The current art world looks for single-authored works. We see works made by one person selling for more money. I believe this stems from a deeply rooted sense of independence and individuality that has emerged in our society during modern times. During the Renaissance, however, multiple artists worked on a project that was attributed to the master of a workshop: perhaps the team was not indicated, but it was understood that many hands were at work.

Imagine this: You live in Renaissance Italy—let's say Florence. You need to produce an image of your wife who passed away to preserve her memory: the way to do that is through portraiture. (Think of how we use photographs of people now: in the same way, portraits were used to commemorate the legacy of people, among other reasons.) You make your way into the workshop of Domenico Ghirlandaio, commission your portrait, and now you wait. What was understood at the time, though, was that his assistants might work on, contribute to, or make the portrait. This is a bit different from our modern idea of commissioning a work. Because our modern idea conflicts with what was generally accepted at

---

1   Sydney Welch, "An Analysis of the Attribution of the Louvre Abu Dhabi Salvator Mundi." (Undergraduate thesis, Arcadia University, 2020).

that time, we sometimes impose our ideas of authorship onto the Renaissance, which can then cloud our ability to analyze the collaborative practices that were in place.

Examples of this workshop process are increasingly rare today. The likelihood of a painting having one author, as we understand artwork today, was less common during the Renaissance because of the workshop tradition. Returning to this glorious tradition of collaboration may lead creators into a renaissance of our own, one where we embrace teamwork and the exchange of ideas and relinquish some of our independence and individuality to collectively elevate our creations.

"Many people are surprised to learn that Leonardo created work with other people and that work attributed to him may never have touched his hands at all."

SYDNEY WELCH

The sale of the *Salvator Mundi* and the new scholarship surrounding its authenticity raises important questions about authorship and the value of creative ownership. Many people are surprised to learn that Leonardo created work with other people and that work attributed to him may never have touched his hands at all.[2] What mattered to members of the court who commissioned these works was the *style* of

2   Ibid.

Leonardo, not so much the presence of his hand. It was even common for works made by his followers and assistants to be passed off as the master's own works. The Italian Renaissance workshop allowed for a looser definition of authorship, and for many that understanding has shifted over time.

The world is becoming increasingly independent as we move further into the age of technology. We see that individuals can accomplish more things quicker and with less help from other people. This easily achievable independence is thanks to apps, YouTube videos, and, of course, Google. Americans in particular have a deep sense of individuality and independence that has roots in the very foundation of our country. A great deal of this individuality in Americans stems from the documents that define our national identity, like the Constitution and the Declaration of Independence. Those documents were created hundreds of years ago, but their messages are still revered in American society to this day. We subconsciously absorb these ideas into the fabric of our nation through standards like school systems, national holidays, and the media.

This subconscious understanding of individuality, I believe, inhibits our ability to embrace something as powerful as collaboration. It imposes a limitation on ourselves and our potential to create *more*. We can achieve a lot by ourselves: we can create really impressive and important things, even, but when we collaborate, what we can achieve is greatness. In writing this book, my hope is to demonstrate to any creator, innovator, entrepreneur, artist, or professional the importance of understanding the value of collaboration and what it looks like for their own pursuits. There is not one way to collaborate: in fact, collaboration looks very different depending on your endeavor. Because of this, I think it is important to look at many different examples of successful collaboration and find ways to incorporate them into our own work.

When it comes to collaborative processes, single-authored works have higher price tags. This reinforces the idea that independence pays off. When someone asks, "Who is the artist?" they probably anticipate one person. This applies significantly to the fine arts, but obviously it is not a one-size-fits-all expectation, because certain industries, like film, have many people involved; but even in some sense the "credit" is given to the director, who is usually one person. This idea that creators, innovators, or artists work alone limits the possibility to elevate creative potential. That is disheartening, given that any random person would probably have decided they aren't an "artist" by middle school because their art projects don't look the way they think they should. Somehow, creativity is understood as a niche and left only to certain types of people. If someone doesn't have that inherent creativity or talent, then they can't create. But they can…

"I want to really challenge the idea that you have to identify as a creative person to create."

SYDNEY WELCH

Creative work can be made possible if it becomes a collaborative act. The ability to collaborate goes against some of these aforementioned ideals that are ingrained in society but embracing collaboration could allow the creative potential of the "average joe" to skyrocket. I want to really challenge the idea that you have to identify as a creative person to create. There is no reason a single-authored work should cost more, and by challenging that notion of authorship by embracing collaboration, we see the potential to turn a corner on the current state of the creative world. Alone, we can achieve a lot, but together we can achieve *more.*

If you enter the world of auction houses and museums and engage in conversations about the Renaissance, it is understood as a "golden age" of creativity. What is sometimes left out from that narrative is the degree of collaboration that was involved. We are in a world that is constantly shifting and changing, and we have access to information, people, and resources in a way that has never before existed. This access destroys the barriers to collaboration and makes it easier than ever. The Renaissance was viewed as a rebirth of ideas and a revival of the ancient techniques that were forgotten over time. Perhaps collaboration has been forgotten or, at the very least, has been underutilized. The opportunity to emerge into our own renaissance is among us, and we need to revive collaboration.

There is so much power in collaboration, and I believe collaborative work leads to the greatest outcome with the biggest impact. Collaboration is an opportunity to pull ideas together from different people to break outside the box. If you are working in a collaborative setting, there is a lot to learn; if you are trying to begin a collaborative project, there is a lot to learn. Anyone looking to harness their creativity and break free from the status quo will benefit from the experience of the network of creators within these pages. This book could be great for educators, teachers, trainers, coaches, and anyone who works with people in a collaborative setting—either for entertainment purposes (art or sports) or for business. This book will discuss how creativity and potential can be unlocked when people work together to achieve goals.

So many impressive creators have shared their insights and stories with me, and these pages are overflowing with important ideas and philosophies that can guide you into collaborations of your own. I spoke with Michael Hartman, a fitness and lifestyle coach, who shared how he harnessed collaboration to avoid competition with other businesses. You will hear from Jill Pederson, an incredible art historian, whose journey into her professional career was inspired and guided by a series of trusted mentors and role models. DJ Okoro shares how keeping his passion just that—a passion— makes collaboration possible and powerful. Amy Voloshin, an inspiring entrepreneur, and I dove into what collaboration looks like for an introvert and how she has navigated starting and running multiple businesses when she values her quiet and alone time. I guarantee you will find someone in this book whose story you can relate to, and you will learn from them how collaboration can take your creation to the next level.

"We are at a point where we can consciously choose to create our own golden age."

SYDNEY WELCH

Returning to this tradition of collaboration that we see in the Renaissance is an incredible opportunity that may lead us into a renaissance of our own. The Renaissance creators we revere did not necessarily create anything new; they were simply reimagining and reviving ideas from antiquity that they thought were valuable and had been lost or forgotten. We now have the opportunity to re-revive those same ideas. We are at a point where we can consciously choose to create our own golden age, one where we embrace teamwork and the exchange of ideas and let go of some of our independence and individuality to collaboratively elevate our creations. During the Renaissance, those innovators and creators were aware of big changes happening. Society was shifting in a remarkable way—but only afterwards came the acknowledgment of how powerful those shifts were. We can deliberately enter our renaissance and document, discuss, and create it with intention and collaboration.

LEONARDO DA VINCI AND THE ITALIAN RENAISSANCE WORKSHOP

———

Traditionally, when we think of visual artists, only the big names make their way to the record. This probably has something to do with how projects have an opportunity to make a social impact. Visual culture is as dominant now as it was in the Renaissance. In the same way the Medici family lined the streets of Florence with their family crest, Coca-Cola has capitalized on the branding of Santa Claus.[3] It's the same story with different characters.

When we look back at the Renaissance, visual culture was just as prominent as today's symbols and logos: except instead of

---

3   The Coca-Cola Company, "Did Coca-Cola Create Santa Claus?: The Coca-Cola Company." https://www.coca-colacompany.com/faqs/did-coca-cola-invent-santa.

posters, it was paintings. You can see how the manual labor required for a painting results in mass production being nearly impossible. During the Renaissance, the printing press hadn't even celebrated its centennial. So as we begin to analyze Leonardo and his workshop, we have to understand that his ability to fulfill commissions was limited simply by time and very little opportunity to change something once it was finished. Now, with websites like Patreon, creators can crowdfund and use different tools to control their brand and be selective about what commissions meet their mission.

Leonardo da Vinci, arguably the most famous artist in the world, is known for his collaborative efforts. The most important and expensive paintings in the world emerged from a workshop setting that is less common in today's practice. There has been a great shift of reliance on the community to the individualistic American mindset, which in a lot of ways compromises the ability to collaborate. The High Renaissance, which is often referred to as the Golden Age, suggests the peak of human creation and innovation and the revival of and improvement upon the best techniques from antiquity. Now is our time to do it again.

We are facing an opportunity to embark into a neo-Renaissance by embracing collaboration and changing the narrative around authorship. Newer artists don't always have the voice or platform to advocate for themselves and their talents, but collaborative efforts with bigger names can help them gain the exposure and momentum to jumpstart their careers. Look at Lil Dicky, for example: he was producing popular music in the Philly suburbs for a while, but it wasn't until 2018, when he released "Freaky Friday" featuring Chris Brown, that his career really took off. Then, in 2019, he released "Earth," which featured a ton of musicians and actors.[4] These collaborations brought his name into the media's attention because he was associated with these other celebrities, built relationships with them, and eventually collaborated on work with them.

"During the Italian Renaissance, it was common for artists to have multiple people working with them in their workshops to produce one commission."

SYDNEY WELCH

The idea of collaborative work can be traced throughout history. The specific point in history I want to highlight as a pinnacle of collaborative success is the Italian Renaissance and the tradition of the Italian Renaissance workshop. During the Italian Renaissance, it was common for artists to have multiple people working with them in their workshops to produce one commission. In terms of producing paintings, jobs were delegated: one person had the task of cutting wood, someone else had to stretch and prepare the canvas, etc. We see this tradition permeate the courtly culture during the Renaissance.

This is a prime example of how collaboration led to success and faster production of work. I want to apply the idea that

---

4   David Jeffries, "Lil Dicky: Biography & History," AllMusic. https://www.allmusic.com/artist/lil-dicky-mn0003400565/biography.

"many hands make light work" to modern times. I believe there is such a push for individualism that people are neglecting to utilize a simple tool that is always available: collaboration. Why are we relying so heavily on ourselves to complete something all on our own when we can utilize the strengths of others?

When analyzing the available evidence used to authenticate any artwork, it is crucial to define what constitutes someone as the author or artist. This is particularly crucial when discussing works that may have been created in a workshop of a master. The primary time period where we see examples of this is during the Renaissance. Leonardo himself studied as an apprentice under Verrocchio, and many works that emerged from the workshop of Verrocchio include work done by the hand of Leonardo.[5] Verrocchio was a master sculptor and also completed commissions for paintings. It is interesting for many people to learn that Leonardo, the master painter, was brought up as an artist in a studio that was primarily producing sculpture. The amount of involvement by either the master or the apprentice varies greatly, and this highlights one of the challenges in defining authorship for works emerging from Renaissance workshops. As artists grew in popularity, commissions increased, and the extent to which the masters executed the work becomes increasingly challenging to decipher.[6] This concept challenges art historians and presents a specific problem in the case of the art museums

---

5   Laurence Kanter, Leonardo: Discoveries from Verrochio's Studio: Early Paintings and New Attributions (New Haven, CT: Yale University Press, 2018) n.p.

6   Sydney Welch, "An Analysis of the Attribution of the Louvre Abu Dhabi Salvator Mundi." (Undergraduate thesis, Arcadia University, 2020). N.p.

and the art market, which often look to promote singularly autographed works.

As most renowned artists did at the time, Leonardo took on pupils of his own. His own training as an artist began under Andrea del Verrocchio, and it is not uncommon to see works with an attribution to both the master Verrocchio and his pupil Leonardo.[7] In the same tradition, it is reasonable to understand that Leonardo worked alongside his pupils on many commissions, where after close observation, both hands are visibly present.

He took ages to complete paintings, so he would delegate tasks to his pupils in his workshop: "Leonardo would sometimes correct or 'finish' [the paintings]." "Given Leonardo's notoriously slow rate of production, this alone explains Bandello's characterization of the typical Milanese palace as having a painting by Leonardo hanging within it, paintings which might not have been executed by him, but which could nonetheless be treated as 'his.'"[8]

In reference to Leonardo's portraits, Luke Syson indicates that Leonardo's style "establishes a model for the Leonardesque portrait."[9] Because the popularity of the style of Leonardo took off in Milan, many Milanese courtiers under Ludovico Sforza yearned to have work by the master himself hanging on their walls. "The style and format of these pictures were

7   Ibid.

8   Luke Syson, "Leonardo and Leonardism in Renaissance Milan," in Artists at Court, ed. Stephen J Campbell (Boston, Isabella Stewart Gardner Museum, 2004), pp. 106-123.

9   Ibid.

much imitated," and the artisans in Milan rapidly adopted his techniques and so began the production of work in the style of Leonardo.[10] "Encouraged by the political situation, and partly as a response to the pressure of work on Leonardo himself, painters already working in Milan learned Leonardo's technique. Going on to re-employ his motifs in their own works to create a new, identifiably Lombard school of painting, a style that significantly originated with Leonardo and Lodovico il Moro."[11]

In the same way that Coca-Cola created our modern idea of Santa Claus, Leonardo created a style of portraiture that was then replicated in a crazy amount in Milan. At the time, the *style* of Leonardo could sell *as* a Leonardo, and the *style* was more important than the actual artist. This is so much different from our modern practice, where the value is in the autograph.

When we get into it, it's clear that the Renaissance was extremely collaborative in nature in a way we may not initially understand today. This is hugely important to understand, because in the Renaissance tradition, Leonardo and his style were so greatly desired by courtiers that "individual style was transformed into a collective one, and the artist himself became a kind of multiple...if those adopting his style should be classified as imitators, rather than as collaborators whose own individual craft and talent were absorbed within the

---

10   Sydney Welch, "An Analysis of the Attribution of the Louvre Abu Dhabi Salvator Mundi." (Undergraduate thesis, Arcadia University, 2020).

11   Luke Syson, "Leonardo and Leonardism in Renaissance Milan," in Artists at Court, ed. Stephen J Campbell (Boston,: Isabella Stewart Gardner Museum, 2004), pp. 106-123.

famous master's artistic personality."[12] This was not seen as forgery, but rather as imitation of a desired style, and to that note, I question why we have trouble with this concept in modern times.

Knowing that Leonardo was widely imitated and also understanding the nature of his collaborative practices highlights the very idea that this book aims to suggest. Collaboration was a tool employed in the Renaissance, the Golden Age of human innovation, so in order to embark on our own renaissance, we must utilize this practice and revive collaboration and these workshop practices.

---

12   Ibid.

THE MODERN WORKSHOP TRADITION WITH BOBBY CLOUGHEN

———

Many people are surprised to learn that the workshop tradition Leonardo da Vinci and his pupils partook in actually still exists to this day. It has changed and evolved over time, but artists are still in their workshops with studio assistants and pupils working with them on their projects in a collaborative fashion. Bobby Cloughen, apprentice of American abstract artist Ed Kerns, is an excellent example of this persistent tradition. Kerns is one of the last remaining artists of his generation of Abstract Expressionist painters, which includes James Brooks, Ernest Briggs, and William de Kooning.[13] Cloughen took a painting class on a whim in college and ended up with Kerns as his professor. They got along well, and Kerns offered Bobby a job as his studio assistant in the

---

13   Ed Kerns, "About," Ed Kerns, accessed October 11, 2020, https://edkernsart.com/about-1.

summer. Bobby had a unique experience as a non-art student, but his experience as an apprentice in a studio is deeply rooted in traditions that date back to the Renaissance.

The tradition of apprenticeship encourages collaboration. Students learn from the master before going off and embracing their own style while having had some degree of formal training within the studio. Cloughen began thinking about his own artistic processes and realized that until his time with Ed, he was not formally trained. The experience Bobby had is a bit different from many other artists who are formally trained for years, but what I find energizing about his story is the lack of formal training. In our chat, Cloughen shared, "For lots of artists, you have to practice for years, refine your technique, and make something 'beautiful,' but what I'm doing when I paint is allowing the image to turn out however it does; my whole idea is rooted in expressing some sort of feeling or emotion that I need to express, and I do that with the actual strokes of paint. I do it in a really simple way. These paintings are more of an expression of a personal freedom. I start picking colors and repetitive techniques, and this is a process I adopted directly from Ed."

Bobby was immediately drawn to Kerns and his personality and approach to painting. Bobby, like many people, fell into the school of thought that artists were reclusive and introverted, but as he got to know Kerns, he realized Kerns had a big personality and brought that into his artwork. "I was so drawn to that, and I couldn't understand how he was so competent in his work and still so informal in conversation as a professional artist. He is the opposite: he says things so simply, which encouraged me to just make art and not feel that fear." A lot of creators grapple with this feeling of fear that arises when creating something new. "I was scared because I didn't want to ruin the painting or mess it up." Bobby said Kerns really helped him get over that fear: "Ed would give me paint and tell me to do something. He had me working on his paintings with such ease. He would tell me to paint something blue and I would just do it to his work. I always thought painting was so delicate, and that's really why I never thought I had a place in that tradition." As Bobby was learning from Kerns in his studio, he was also seeing so many stereotypes and preconceived notions completely disappear.

As Bobby was settling into his work with Ed, he began understanding the power of his process. "I am surrounded by these big paintings, and they aren't small gestures. He would tell me to pour an entire cup of paint on the canvas, and after I got over those nerves, I began to feel an amazing sensation of control. I stepped into this world that was out of control and I had no vision. Most of the time I didn't know what Ed was talking about, and by the end of the summer, Ed and I were calibrated. We were thinking ahead and sometimes even making the same moves." The role of the apprentice is really important to help articulate an idea I proposed in the introduction: relinquishing our independence to embrace a collective. Generally speaking, an apprentice's name is not put on their master's painting, even though they worked on it together. We have this desire to receive credit for our work, so a lot of people struggle with the idea of collaboration because the credit shifts. Bobby was not fazed by this at all. "It's all Ed's work, but maybe those four hundred dots on the painting were made by me. There is no part of this work that made me question if I got adequate credit: I'm his apprentice.

I met amazing people, I got paid well, and I did my job as his apprentice and assistant. This world is very much established, and there is a formal and right way to do it, and seventy-five years into his life, he was not doing it the wrong way."

"Although I was in a different building, in a different world, I felt completely in touch with the tradition of the Italian Renaissance workshop."

BOBBY CLOUGHEN

I think Bobby has a great grasp on the workshop tradition and his role in it while working with Ed. Bobby worked on pieces with Ed for Ed's shows, but he also had the opportunity to create his own work. "I got the chance to completely take things over on some of the paintings and they became mine. Collaboration was essential, because with a lot of works, they started out as Ed Kerns' and completed as mine." We see examples of this from pupils, even of Leonardo da Vinci... "Although I was in a different building, in a different world, I felt completely in touch with the tradition of the Italian Renaissance workshop. Although it has evolved so much, I felt like I was a part of this great age of modern painting. Sometimes we would just talk for hours: we would make coffee and talk, and no painting would get done. That was just part of the process." Everything Ed has encountered in his long life brings something to his artwork. In the same way, Bobby has a lot to offer as someone who has lived a different experience than Ed. They have a lot to learn from each other, and this exchange of ideas is so powerful and fundamental to collaboration. Every human being is already a work of collaboration. We are a sum of our parts and experiences. Throughout our lives, we constantly choose what we like from every person who comes into our lives and adopt and adjust those things to work for us. This is certainly the case for apprentices in a workshop, as it is for any person. It's important to understand that whether or not we choose to embrace or use the term, we are *already* collaborating constantly.

THE SCIENCE OF COLLABORATION

———

"According to 'Understanding the Psychology of Guilt' on Eruptingmind.com, most children were taught from a young age to seek approval from their parents for the things they said or did. Since the need for approval, love and acceptance from our parents is strong, we become conditioned over time to seek approval from others as well."[14] Over time, this need for approval can shift our ideas, our titles, and ultimately our careers. It's a natural part of human development, but one that might inhibit our ability to successfully collaborate. I believe part of successful collaboration is letting go of the need for "credit" or individual praise, given that the nature of collaboration is working together as a team. This relies on "unlearning" our need for validation and teaching ourselves to feel that same sense of accomplishment from a collaborative success.

———

14   Lauren Suval, "What Drives Our Need For Approval?," World of Psychology, July 8, 2018, https://psychcentral.com/blog/what-drives-our-need-for-approval/.

A recently published *Forbes* article echoes this idea as it talks about eliminating titles in the workplace. "The concept of no titles naturally sparks one's ego to make counter arguments because you will no longer be special. Put your ego aside and consider how much more collaborative and flexible work would be if you didn't waste your time with a job title but got excited about multiple roles or responsibilities."[15] This highlights the fact that collaboration and ego do not pair well. The ego looks for titles, distinctions, praise, and credit, whereas collaboration is more about the end goal and focusing on creating the best possible version of your vision. Collaboration works in the same way that team sports require working together and knowing when to step in and when to step back. Contribute your part and allow others to do the same. Power-hungry people have no place in collaboration because it is not about controlling the vision, but rather elevating the vision by maxing out everyone's creative potential.

All of this information might make it seem like collaboration is not widely utilized or regarded by professionals and in workspaces, but here are some statistics to help situate collaboration in the current state of the professional world.

- "Roughly 75% of employees regard collaboration and teamwork as important.

- 39% of a survey's respondents felt that their company could collaborate more.

---

15   Gabriel Tupula, "Council Post: Position Over Title: Increasing Collaboration In The Workplace," Forbes (Forbes Magazine, June 19, 2020), https://www.forbes.com/sites/forbesbusinesscouncil/2020/06/22/position-over-title-increasing-collaboration-in-the-workplace/.

- Collaboration is in the top four important skills for employees' future success.

- Over 60% of Generation X and Millennials would collaborate more through visual means.

- Online collaboration tools and digital workplaces facilitate increased productivity by up to 30%."[16]

Seventy-five percent of employees recognize the importance of collaboration and teamwork, so it is important to offer employees opportunities to work on projects in small groups. Thirty-nine percent of employees felt their companies could collaborate more, which shows there is space to increase collaboration: but even in spaces where it is being utilized, it can definitely be improved upon.

In order to dive into an entire book about collaboration, it's important to first define what it even means. I would encourage you, before reading the definition that I will be providing, to consider what your definition or preconceived idea about collaboration is.

According to Merriam-Webster, the definition of *collaborate* is as follows:

"*intransitive verb*

---

16 Raj Vardhman, et al. "24+ Mesmerizing Workplace Collaboration Statistics for 2020," goremotely, September 9, 2020, https://goremotely. net/blog/workplace-collaboration/.

1. to work jointly with others or together especially in an intellectual endeavor

2. to cooperate with or willingly assist an enemy of one's country and especially an occupying force

3. to cooperate with an agency or with which one is not immediately connected. instrumentality with which one is not immediately connected."[17]

So now we know what the *typical* definition of collaboration is. What you will come to learn as you read on is that I am pushing this definition to its limits. I am stretching and pulling and reshaping what we have come to understand collaboration to be and trying to find out what it can look like for different people in different settings. Everyone should collaborate—it's the way forward—but this simple definition might not be enough to get people off the ground. So as we move through this book you will get tangible examples from successful collaborators about what it looks like in their endeavors.

---

17 "Collaboration," Merriam-Webster (Merriam-Webster), accessed October 11, 2020, https://www.merriam-webster.com/dictionary/collaboration.

MY COLLABORATIVE
EXPERIENCE

———

As an art history major, I became intimate with the complicated ideas surrounding authorship and attribution sparked
by the *Salvator Mundi*. I initially felt challenged by how credit
was given to different artists. I began to develop a deeper
understanding of these processes alongside my first major
experience with collaboration. I was a freshman at Arcadia
University, and I hadn't declared my major yet, but I was
leaning toward an art major. When I saw the opportunity
to participate something called the Arcadia Public Art Project, I was immediately interested and noted that freshmen
weren't actually able to participate. I had to go petition and
get advisors to recommend me, but I ended up getting to
participate in it as a first-year student. Having those advisors
advocate for and reassure me that I could join this project
was really one of those "make-or-break" moments that I have
been able to witness in retrospect. I joined the project and
began working as an apprentice under David Guinn. David,
a group of students, and I planned and designed a mural at

a local underpass near the train station. The first year, we hit a lot of road bumps and learned so much from them, but we never ceased to have conversations about how things were going, where the money was coming from, and how the mural would be put up on the wall. Something else that was very clear was that despite our different roles in the project, we all shared the ownership of the finished piece.

Most of the students who were working on the project were art students or fine art students, so they were making art, and I was leaning toward art history and the philosophy of art, as well as the more curatorial, business and entrepreneurship side. So initially I was a little bit intimidated to be working on a mural, but then I started taking shape with the project and having a role in it. I was able to use my interest in entrepreneurship to raise money and do project management and coordination. So at first it was a little bit intimidating, but ultimately, I got to use my unique skill set to advance the project.

We started this incredible project that the community was really excited about. I was able to coordinate community meetings to get the community's input, and then we would have group meetings with the artists and the students. Then we got into the process of planning out the mural and making sure it was something everyone had a role in. I don't think we would have had the same outcome and success we were met with if we hadn't had the community's ideas come to the table in conjunction with my entrepreneurship and business skills and the art skills of the other students. Of course, the cherry on top was the incredible advising from David Guinn, the famous muralist who we were working with. It was this incredible conglomeration of skills, ideas, and contributions that none of us could have done alone. We were all able to draw upon our strengths to have the project happen quickly and efficiently.

I worked on the second round of the mural project the following year and found that the second time around, we were much more prepared having learned from our mistakes the first year. We collaborated between the projects and found ways to make the murals cohesive but still individual. Aside from David, myself, and one other student, our team was entirely new, which meant our collaboration methods needed to adjust to accommodate our new team.

For me, that project really embodied collaboration every step of the way—from the fundraising, to the community outreach, to the designing and implementation of the public works of art. I learned quickly how important it was to collaborate and saw those efforts culminate in an incredibly successful result that I drive by every day. Now, I sit on the steering committee for the project, and it is a privilege and an honor to be contributing to the continuous effort to create public art.

That experience allowed me to really collaborate and see how important collaboration is to creative success. It is one of the initial experiences that inspired me to write this book, and it helped me make the connections to get started. David was one of the first people I reached out to when I began writing, and you will hear from him and a bit about his experience with the Arcadia Public Art Project. I have experienced collaboration firsthand and can testify to its necessity in creative endeavors. Now, you can hear from others who feel the same way.

PART TWO

TOOLS FOR SUCCESSFUL COLLABORATION

My family and extended family all have pretty cohesive ideas around politics, religion, and the general "issues." I think a lot of families find that they share general ideals, though not all. It adheres to the philosophy that you are the product of the people you surround yourself with. Growing up, I always heard a lot of the same ideas. I am grateful for those—they have brought me to where I am—but as I got older and went off to school, I began to hear different ideas. I started challenging many of the beliefs I grew up with. Regardless of your political affiliation or stance on the "issues," I want to share a story with you about my cousin.

One afternoon in April of this year, my cousin Tom was at my apartment with my brother and our friend Mckenzie. We got into a conversation about politics, and it became obviously quickly that we were on opposing sides of the political spectrum. Mckenzie challenged Tom's views. When someone challenges something you hold to be true, it is uncomfortable, and many people immediately get defensive. Tom is pretty good about *not* doing this, and I hope that anyone reading this book, if nothing else, will remember this story. The conversation shifted and there was definitely some discomfort in the air. Picking up takeout diffused the tension, and shortly after, we parted ways.

A few days later, Tom called me and said he had spent hours researching various aspects of Mckenzie's arguments. He started Googling, watching videos, reading articles, and listening to podcasts, and he was aggressively trying to understand why Mckenzie did not share his political views. He eventually identified some areas where he was misinformed, and he actually saw where Mckenzie was coming from. He then adjusted his viewpoint accordingly. Does he 100 percent agree with Mckenzie now? Definitely not. Did he take the time to understand where she was coming from and LEARN something that changed what he believed? YES!

This is one small example of a much bigger picture in regard to not only being a collaborator but being a successful human being. It is inevitable that you will find people in your life who you care about yet disagree with on one topic or another. You will encounter people who have ideas that are nothing like yours, as all of our lived experiences are so vastly different. It is true you will have to navigate many different challenges in order to see eye-to-eye with these people in your life, but it is possible, and the outcome can be remarkable. We should never be so attached to an idea that we aren't willing to hear other ones.

The next time you find yourself in conversation with a person with different views, try to take the time to understand where they are coming from. It is likely they have information that you do not. Before becoming defensive and attempting to defend your own point of view, ask yourself how this person reached this conclusion. Ask yourself what aspects of their opinion bring value to your own. In a creative setting, ask how their knowledge and opinions can elevate the collective creation.

Part Two will walk you through various tools to navigate collaborative efforts. These tools come from successful creatives who successfully implemented these ideas into their own collaborations.

NAVIGATING COLLABORATIVE CONFLICTS WITH BEETLE CAMPBELL

Conflict in collaboration is inevitable. It is impossible to get along with every person you will ever work with. As I spoke with Beetle Campbell, an independent media and film developer, he shared his stories of collaboration with me, but he didn't hold back on the various examples of conflict that have come up in his career. Conflict has a negative connotation, but perhaps by diving into the experiences Beetle has had and by understanding his perspective we can challenge that connotation.

Beetle began working in video production when he went into the business with his cousin. "It taught me a lot about the market and how to work with clients, but I wasn't able to necessarily go do the things I wanted." This is the nature of working for someone else: you have to adhere to their vision of the company. This "conflict" could be seen negatively, but Beetle adjusted his perspective. Instead of viewing this conflict between his goals and the goals of the company, he saw it as a stepping-stone. He decided to take what he learned from his time with his cousin graciously and leave the company in pursuit of his passions.

"Once I left that company I started working with travel, luxury, and lifestyle brands. Initially, it was just about creating content, and as I continued doing that, I started elevating my career and going up and up." Beetle's initial discomfort in his position ended up pushing him toward a different career path. By identifying what he did *not* want to do in his job, he was able to figure out what he wanted to do.

It's important to note that conflicts can come up in so many different capacities as you embrace collaboration. But you should remember to analyze your perspective and figure out what that conflict is telling you about your next steps. For Beetle, it meant it was time to make a change and work for himself. For others, it might mean something smaller, like a conversation to define roles. While conflict should not be feared, there are a lot of tools you can utilize to have successful collaboration and avoid serious conflicts.

Beetle began utilizing his network to get his foot in the door with the types of companies he was hoping to work with. Those connections helped him make the right connections, "but it was up to [him] to prove [him]self." He was learning how to tailor each project specifically to his clients, and he was able to identify right off the bat what the companies and clients wanted. He was refining his style and ability to cater to his clients in a collaborative way. "It depends on what type of things the companies are after and if they want marketing, photography, adverts, etc. It varies project to project how I work with each client, and I have to come up with something to offer and see if they're interested." This step in his career was crucial to being able to be versatile—something that comes up later in this book—while still maintaining a unique style that is how he markets himself.

All of this work brought Beetle to Africa for fifty days to generate content with other creators. "The entire trip was a collaboration: we were creating so much media. I met a lot of creators who had clients on the trips and were taking photos and creating media for their clientele. All of that time with different creators led me to submit my photos to various magazines and catalogs and culminated in my work being featured on BBC Earth as one of the youngest photographers ever to be featured on their page." That feature evolved from collaboration and getting to know the right people. After this feature, Beetle had various magazines reaching out to him and contacting him about his work. This one trip propelled him in the right direction for the next six months.

After this relatively conflict-free trip to Africa, Beetle was back looking for his next move. He was still feeling the momentum from the trip, but he also started feeling the pressure to get to the next step in his career. His latest work in 2020 took him to the Caribbean. Beetle joined a startup that was looking for someone to create marketing content. He worked on a team of three. He was an outsider brought in to help create content, while the others he worked with were establishing themselves in the new company. This varied amount of "stake in the game" could lead to conflict, but there is a lot to learn from the way Beetle approached these creative differences.

"Of course we clashed heads, mostly because we all had our own unique visions and had to bring them together, which requires someone to sacrifice part of their vision." This is what I believe is the most challenging part of collaboration. I believe no idea is "bad," but some are more effective, cohesive, feasible, or logical. The nature of collaboration includes bringing a bunch of ideas together, while some have to be left behind if they don't serve the bigger mission. So as Beetle articulated, how do you decide whose idea to drop? I think the way Beetle approached this type of collaboration in a professional setting is very clever.

"I was hired to be a videographer and offer my creative input to help engage the company's audience, so I needed to hear what the company was saying, but I also needed to put my twist on things: that's why I was hired, and that's what I am known for." Beetle was hired for a reason—his style appealed to the company. Making sure he didn't sacrifice his style while meeting the expectations and the vision of the company was crucial. "Ultimately, the boss is right, and you need to adjust your work to deliver what they want. A big piece of that is being able to put aside your ego and recognize when your vision isn't resonating with your clients." When you are hired, you report to your boss, so while collaboration can definitely happen, you still have to do your job the way your boss wants it to be done. In the same way that Beetle took the conflict from his first job as a sign to move onto something new, he understood the power dynamic between working for yourself and taking on clients or being hired and working for someone else.

Navigating conflict is extremely important because, as I previously articulated, it does not need to be a bad thing. Conflict is a tool to develop professionalism and a sign that something is not working. In that way, conflict is a great opportunity to learn and evolve. Beetle articulated how he harnessed the various conflicts he has faced to make his style easily adaptable to all different types of clients. "I know my style, and all I need to do is adjust it to each client and situation. If you have generated a style that works across the board, you can apply that to each project and only need to adjust a little bit." One of the most important tools to combat conflict is flexibility. "Working in various companies and sometimes feeling frustrated in the roles I was in and not being able to fulfill the vision that I had taught me how to respect my boss and fight for what I wanted to achieve professionally." This is an important part of professionalism that conflict can bring about. "I knew what I really wanted, but I had to go the other direction for a while, and what I learned was to balance that vision of company and personal vision and goals. When I left that position, I knew what I wanted to achieve and how I wanted to achieve that." As we begin to navigate the importance of flexibility and versatility, keep in mind how the tools in the upcoming chapters help to negate potential conflicts.

UTILIZING EMOTIONAL INTELLIGENCE WITH EMMA BEVERIDGE AND LIVI ANDREINI

Emma Beveridge and Livi Andreini graduated from Wake Forest University in 2020. During their senior year, they were on the leadership team for the Wake Forest University TEDx program. Emma decided to challenge herself, and she became the executive producer for the program. Her junior year roommate, Livi, had worked on the program all throughout her time at Wake Forest and was looking at stepping back a bit for senior year, as the event is very demanding. Emma expressed interest in working on the event with her roommate and fell into her new role seamlessly. As one of the largest entirely student-run TEDx conference events, Emma and Livi were planning for an event that historically has seen crowds of up to two thousand people. Their goal was to unite Winston-Salem, North Carolina and Wake Forest and to create a ripple effect of positive change within the community. You can see why I have chosen to speak with the pair about their experience: from their initial involvement in the conference to pulling it off, the entire event was a huge collaboration.

"It was the first experience I had running something this large without a supervisor. I was the executive producer, working under Livi, the executive director. If we didn't figure it out, it would not happen, so it was a good test of problem solving and working in teams," Emma shared. She and Livi began reaching out to professionals to potentially present at the conference and thus stepped outside of their student identities and into professional ones. "We didn't want to seem like students, and so we put on a professional hat and learned to articulate our numbers, our roles, and regulations. It was a big growth experience in professionalism and maturity," Emma shared.

> "We realized that our emotional check-ins had successfully led us to create a great team that we had spoken about creating months prior."

EMMA BEVERIDGE

Emma was responsible for a team of six executives, and through their collective teams, forty-five volunteers as well as the eight visiting speakers. "When we were reaching out to speakers, I focused on editing a lot of the language we used, and then when we did have speakers for the event, I worked with them one-on-one with their storytelling and writing support." The process was intense, but Emma's emotional intelligence helped her get through it. Both Emma and Livi had to navigate leading a team of their peers while planning this event. Naturally, people feel emotionally attached to their ideas and especially to their speeches and contributions to a big event. In the same way that the volunteers were striving to offer the best ideas to set themselves apart, it was important for Emma to make sure the ideas they moved forward with matched the vision of the event. This could cause hurt feelings or disappointment among coworkers and volunteers. Emma and Livi shared how their emotional intelligence helped them navigate these challenging situations:

"Emotional intelligence was at the foundation of our success with this event. It's why we began to have emotional check-ins." Emma and Livi sat down over the summer and laid out what their emotional needs were, what their leadership styles were, what kind of team they needed, what kind of people they wanted, and what kind of mood they wanted to set among their team. "Once we finished that meeting, we didn't necessarily discuss it that much, but it helped us be really intentional about how we filled the roles of our executive team. Once those roles were filled with people that we carefully selected, we realized that our emotional check-ins had successfully led us to create a great team that we had spoken about creating months prior." This early check-in when the team consisted of just Emma and Livi really allowed them to set the stage for where they wanted to go in terms of teamwork and collaboration.

Whenever you go into a collaborative setting, it can be really effective to sit down and establish where you want the collaboration to go and what you hope the end goal will be. It can be even more powerful (depending on the length of the project) to pause to see how things are going and to create a space to voice concerns or problems. Emma and her partners did this by having "emotional check-ins." "When we did hit bumps in the road, those emotional check-ins helped us get back on the road to meeting our vision. They set the foundation for getting to our goal, put us back on track when we needed it, and kept us intentional about our work and our decisions," Livi shared. I think the excitement of collaborating, especially in the beginning, could cloud the need for these emotional check-ins. Everyone at the beginning of the project is energized with lots of new ideas and willingness to work but establishing this emotional framework can really help when that momentum slows down or if the project derails.

The regular aspects of a collaborative project, like time management, setting boundaries, and deciding timelines, are all very natural, and people have them as their strong suits. Those skills are important and need to be utilized, but the first skill that is at the core of everything is emotional intelligence. "For me, that allowed me to know when to step in and when to step back." Emma shared a great example of how this helped her resolve a conflict with one of their team members. "One of our members had a creative marketing project that they wanted to do. Her ideas were there, but the follow-through was lacking. She was struggling with how to plan and make the project actually happen. I was able to open up a dialogue with her and discuss where the project was facing problems and how to make it go forward. We set goals and deadlines and set expectations to help make it happen." There is balance that being emotionally intelligent can help you achieve.

Leading a conversation with emotional intelligence in mind allows you to approach issues from a calm state of mind, and it makes you consider the emotional needs of each participant—not just the needs of the project. What does a team need to be successful? What does a team need to feel supported? "I had to figure out how to communicate [my coworker's] weaknesses with kindness and compassion, but I also had to overcome that discomfort that comes naturally with confrontation," Emma said. It was an opportunity to improve an aspect of the project, but it did not require being mean or aggressive: an open conversation solved the issue. Our emotions have the potential to dictate how an entire collaboration can go. Livi shared, "We first always had to check in with ourselves and make sure that we had our emotions together so we could set the tone." The pair set their team up to be leaders, which involved recognizing the strengths of their team, the weaknesses, and the capabilities. Leadership starts with you, and setting the tone for a collaborative project can really make or break it.

KEEPING THE PASSION WITH EAST LOVE MUSIC AND DJ OKORO

———

Rob Fink of the band East Love shared some interesting insights about collaboration with me. East Love is a project in which none of the band members are full-time musicians. Rob is currently in business school and also works on the global marketing team at Spotify. East Love has three main members, Rob, Lucas, and Alex, and have had some other musicians come in and out. These three go all the way back to middle school, and they exemplify how long-lasting collaborations can lead to success. "Lucas has been singing as long as I can remember; he used to sing at the talent show in elementary and middle school. I have been playing guitar since I was eight or nine. Lucas and I became best friends and started playing together, and our idea of fulfilling our community service requirement in high school was playing music at old age homes and rehab centers in our hometown." Sometimes collaborations begin without even realizing it: they can start as a passion project and end up creating something beautiful.

> ## "I was never a singer, but I was musically inclined, so he wanted to start harmonizing when we would play music. He convinced me to start singing."
>
> ROB FINK

East Love began to evolve as Rob, Lucas, and Alex went through high school and started taking their music a little more seriously. "We were in my room playing some music and would record stuff on GarageBand, and Lucas started trying to encourage me to sing. I was never a singer, but I was musically inclined, so he wanted to start harmonizing when we would play music. He convinced me to start singing." Suddenly, the two were collaborating with their voices, and creating new sounds that would later become the basis for their band. They play a lot of pop music but have a unique folk-sounding twist. Alex joined the duo in high school along with another friend, and their makeshift group began to take shape. In their final year of high school, they chose to make their "senior project" creating an original album. They took that time to record their songs with a connection who was a budding producer, and that was really the beginning of where East Love is at now. "Singing together is the foundation of what East Love is."

Naturally, the boys went to different colleges, and their music took a bit of a back seat. They played together over breaks and when they could all get together at home, and the group remained close friends. After graduating, they all moved home to New York and wound up with the current version of the group, and they began to really focus on it and take it seriously. "Our intention was to have fun, so we started a Facebook page where we would make covers and post them. We all had big networks that wanted to come see us, and that's when we saw there was something there and wanted to go for it." They took the big leap to music streaming platforms and some of the other logistics to become a real band, but it didn't happen overnight. They made the decision to have practices, record their music, and put it out to the public. They recognized that people were resonating with their music and messages, but they all continued to pursue other professional careers. This side project still demands countless hours, and it's their passion project.

Collaboration goes hand in hand with passion because whether or not you want to eventually capitalize, passion is what drives collaboration. While most of this book focuses on people in professional business roles, I wanted to include the story of East Love to highlight the importance of *passion*. It's also valuable to recognize that these passion projects don't have to become a career if you don't want them to. You can do it all! You just have to dedicate yourself.

"You cannot effectively create when you are also simultaneously judging what you are creating. You can later go back and scrutinize your work." Rob shared how this is a big struggle for him and how in some ways it's beneficial when the group needs to really refine something. Each member of the group has a unique creative process and creative tendencies. There is no rule to how they create their music. That's important with collaboration: a predefined process is restrictive and limits what can happen, while openness to the progression and evolution of a process is what allows things to form with passion. Rules, in some ways, destroy passion. However, in order to maintain the creations, sometimes deadlines need to be set and subsequently met. "We all have to pull in equal parts because it's just us—we don't have a manager or anything—so we all have to do jobs that we don't like or sometimes feel like we don't have the time to do. This can create tension or frustration. After all of these years—and sometimes it works better than other times—we always arrive back at the same place. We all want to keep it going and we are all passionate about it." When these challenges emerge, they are defeated because of that passion. "At the end of the day, we are doing this to feel good. We always come back to this discussion, where if something is out of balance, sometimes we're not feeling great, but we come back to this discussion where this only works if we are all having a good time and feeling good about what we are putting in and getting out as individuals." No matter what the collaboration is, passion needs to be the driving force to get through the challenges.

Over the years, the members of the band have come and gone, and currently in addition to the core three, Andy and Austin are now part of the East Love crew. The band has evolved, and their creative process has undergone a similar evolution. Any time you bring together different people with different styles and tendencies, collaboration is key. In order to really work together with different people, you need to have a sort of give and take. What can you offer, and what can you adopt? East Love has spent lots of time putting in their individual contributions and then melding them together to create their unique sound. "The idea of collaboration is a very real idea for us and one we couldn't live without, because we know the sum of the parts are greater than the whole." Rob told me how they all have great musical abilities, but when it all comes together, what they create is better than what anyone could achieve individually. This sentiment is the entire basis of this book. Individually, we can achieve. Together, we can elevate these achievements and create things we didn't even know were possible.

DJ OKORO

It's 2015, and my friends and I are approaching the student center at Portsmouth Abbey High School; you can hear the music from outside. The person in charge? Josh Okoro. Josh started DJ-ing in high school at the Abbey, and I have some fond memories from school dances where Josh and his friend Ryan were the DJs of the school dances. "I told my parents about those experiences, and after graduation they got me a DJ board," Josh said. This gift came with a condition, though: Josh's mom said she wanted him to really do something with it and look at it as an investment. "At first, I was terrible, but I was able to get people into my dorm room freshman year of college and set up lights in my room. It was my escape from the stresses of school, and I would mix things together that I liked." Throughout college, Josh began picking up tricks and improving his skills. All of a sudden, his friends started listening to his mixes, which had improved a lot since his freshman dorm parties. Then, one night, Josh met the owner of a bar that he frequented, and his friend got him hired for a night. That was his first gig.

"I went out on a limb and followed through the connection, and they set me up for a demo one night. I remember I was so nervous. I had worked on the set for days before trying to make sure that the crowd liked it." The crowd liked it so much that Josh was hired as a regular. It snowballed, and Josh began getting exposure and more gigs with good reviews, which led him to the point he has reached now. "People were the most important aspect of it, because as much as I love making music for myself, I wanted to create something that other people liked and get that affirmation that I could make something for other people to enjoy." Once Josh got connected with a club DJ, he had a professional who took on a mentor-like role for him and helped him begin fine-tuning his music. Collaborating with professionals as a novice is always a fantastic idea, because if you are willing to, the amount of knowledge you can absorb is endless. Josh shared how getting feedback from listeners is one of his biggest tools to keep improving.

What I think is really unique about Josh and his journey of collaborating with his listeners is that he doesn't do this for his profession. Instead, this is his passion project that he keeps on the side. "In some ways, making music for a profession would compromise my music and my passion. I would have to do performances that may not align with my vision. What I want overall is to be out there and have people enjoy my music." By keeping music as his passion and not his profession, Josh is able to keep it as his escape. "If I made it my profession and always had to focus on making great music, it would stress me out, and I would fall out of love for it." It's important to have this self-awareness of what degree you want your passion to be in your life. Some people have the personality to make it their profession; others want to keep it as a hobby. I think sometimes we forget that it's okay to have hobbies and do something just for the enjoyment and fulfillment we get from it. Josh has a degree in civil engineering, and his career path is in construction management. He said, "It relates a lot to DJ-ing because I still get to have a leadership [role] and control of a situation. It's using two parts of my brain: one side is engineering, and the other side is focused on making music and being a DJ. I want to do both in life." By choosing both, Josh is able to pursue a professional interest and maintain his passion project. He has found a way to maintain the freedom to make music and eliminate the burden of the need to create it that might be present if he made it his career.

There is something really beautiful about being creative and collaborating when the dollar signs are removed. For Josh, his ability to create is never compromised with the stress of income or work burnout. This stressor doesn't always affect everyone, but I think most people can see how stress can corrupt creativity. In reality, stress corrupts everything. It may be worth contemplating whether your stress in life has compromised your ability to innovate, create, and ultimately collaborate. Josh has found an incredible way to be successful creatively and collaboratively without making his passion his full-time job. We saw East Love really embody this same sentiment. Keeping the passion alive is the best way to really show up creatively, energized, and ready to collaborate.

NONVERBAL COLLABORATION WITH KRISTY LEONE

―――

"Sometimes we don't need to have a conversation because we recognize that words may not be the most powerful tool."

KRISTY LEONE

Collaboration can help you articulate something that you might not be able to otherwise. Kristy Leone, an artist and art therapist, has learned to use collaborative arts to support her ability to communicate with clients. Her love of art and curiosity about the human condition made her choice to be an art therapist easy. Kristy is also an artist in her own right and creates incredible pieces of fluid art, which is a technique of painting that she has come to love. Fluid art involves pouring combinations of paint over a canvas and allowing the paint to flow about with some direction from the artist. There are lots of different techniques used in fluid art, and it can be truly mesmerizing to look at. Kristy recognized from her own processes in the arts how healing it was for her, and so the combination of her two big interests led her to her role as the only creative art therapist in her group practice.

Kristy finds counseling to be a very collaborative process in nature. "With counseling, the most crucial part is actually collaborating with others by showing the best care for your client and seeing what you can accomplish with them. Then the next aspect of collaboration in my practice is our weekly group meetings with the other counselors in our practice to discuss the best way to support our clients in a professional and supervised setting." Therapists and counselors have a strong mission to give their clients the best possible help available to them. Something Kristy brought up that I found really fascinating is that sometimes providing the best care for a client means making a referral to another specialist. This may be within their practice, but it could be an outside referral. "It comes from our ethics board: it's about knowing if you can give the best care, and, if not, you have to recognize who is the best person to refer them to. I might not have experience with people going through something, so I refer them to someone who does." Kristy herself even receives referrals from other counselors and therapists. There is a give-and-take process that must be collaborative while still maintaining the sensitivity to respect that privacy. "A lot of the referrals I get derive from clients who have trouble talking, so instead of having to talk, we make art."

Verbalization is not the only way people can tell their story. "They may be resistant to the traditional counseling process, so instead of forcing that on them, we utilize art." The idea that not every story needs to be told verbally is really important and a crucial part of Kristy's story.

Kristy has been able to make great progress with some of her clients because there is an immediate attraction to visual language. Kristy shared that trauma patients respond especially well to art therapy because they are able to take an experience that was really intense and instead of having to verbalize it, they can visualize it. It may be challenging to articulate ideas, and some people are more comfortable showing rather than telling. This directly corresponds to collaboration, because while verbal communication is extremely important, it may not work for everyone. How can you step outside the box and find creative ways to communicate with your team and partners?

"Sometimes we don't need to have a conversation because we recognize that words may not be the most powerful tool." Kristy uses artwork as a means of communication with her clients. "What came up for me is this collaboration between professionals, which tends to happen naturally to some degree, but there is a necessary collaboration that I have with my clients, and I can't do my job effectively unless I am collaborating with them in terms of treatment, goals, and offering them effective care." If we elevate this to the field of collaboration as a whole, it's remarkable to think of what can be achieved if we use varied methods of collaboration—not just collaborative conversation.

Kristy shared with me that one day she was running a group counseling session at a behavioral health center, and a woman approached her and asked what individual art therapy might look like. This woman began sharing with Kristy some of her struggles but said she was feeling stuck trying to articulate them. Kristy took out some art materials and asked the woman to try and show what these feelings looked like.

"What ended up happening was that her feeling kind of looked like a hole, and when we turned it on its side, it looked more like a cave. We explored that idea of these feelings being a cave, and the woman found that a cave isn't so scary. It isn't so scary because it's just a dead-end tunnel and she can still turn around. That moment became a metaphor throughout her treatment: it's not a hole, it's a tunnel."

That use of art as a means of collaboration led one of her clients to visualize her feelings and then reassess what they meant based on how they looked. It's really so powerful in terms of therapy. Think of the possibilities if we incorporate nonverbal collaborations into our own practice. "People carry images and symbols with them, which over time they turn into metaphors or little moments and realizations that help guide them through their anxiety/trauma/depression/ etc." These symbols and uses of images and visual imagery outside the context of counseling could turn into your next logo, advertisement, painting, or project.

"People are defensive sometimes about being creative: maybe someone's only 'art' experience is their elementary art class, so there is a component of resistance that many people have when you try and engage them in the creation of art. The clients that are the most resistant to art making usually will dive into abstract art. This allows them to shift their focus from making perfect forms, looking for a specific goal, to just expressing whatever they are feeling." There is a huge opportunity to learn about collaboration here from Kristy's experiences with various clients and using art as a language to translate and communicate complex ideas and feelings.

DEFINING ROLES
WITH LEAF SHAVE

———

Collaboration involves the bringing together of multiple minds, and in a business setting this can sometimes lead to uneasy power dynamics. In order to successfully collaborate and avoid this issue, defining the roles of each collaborator is important. This idea came up in my conversation with Adam Simone, the CEO of Leaf Shave. Adam Simone started the company with his colleague and friend Adam Hahn. Both of them are engineers and had the vision to create the best shave by reinventing the razor. They work from different states, but their predefined roles have allowed them to successfully run and operate a company together while apart.

Simone and Hahn have complementary skill sets, and they are both engineers, but they had to figure out the best way to work together. They achieved this by laying out their roles right off the bat. Before they did anything, they defined each of their roles within the company and what those looked like to them. That's not to say they didn't both heavily participate in all of the processes: rather, they defined their roles and who was going to make the ultimate decisions for which parts of the company. "Trying to make unanimous decisions deadlocks a business." They respect the other person enough to make the decision in their own roles. "You can't move forward if you don't let each person do what they are supposed to do." Unanimity can work in unique situations, but trying to force it might cause someone to sacrifice part of their vision to achieve the ultimate goal. Agreeing to predefined roles allows for collaborators to make decisions efficiently, even if they aren't entirely unanimous. The deadlock that Simone referred to is something that can seriously slow down the progression of projects.

"Successful collaboration is all about spirited conversation and mutual respect." It happens every day at Leaf Shave, and it really comes down to how you set up how to work together. Simone and Hahn quite literally sat down and laid out the rules. Simone has control of branding and marketing, and Hahn deals with more of the product-design aspects. These predefined roles ended up being important when trying to name the company. With a lot of ideas for potential names for the business, the pair had to define what that name encapsulated and what it said about their company. "A lot of the ideas were innovation heavy: that touched on the natural tech of the razor, and the one I really liked was Leaf. It was subtle and had a nod to how our razor opened and actually worked, but it also gives a bit of a gender-neutral feel and a nod to the environment." They did not agree on the name and went around and around, but ultimately, because of their predefined roles, Simone was able to make the decision with the support of his partner and respect for that role. This perfectly exemplifies an instance where predefined roles assist in the collaborative process.

Having a partner and collaborating with them opens avenues for greater success. "I don't think we could even operate if this was just one of us; the number-one piece of advice I always give entrepreneurs is to find a cofounder." Partnerships allow for a constant discourse and a division of responsibilities, which ultimately takes some of the pressure off of one individual. Partnerships are about supporting one another really well and having the ability to discuss. "We argue all the time in a really friendly way, and through the strengths of our individual opinions, I think we see different options and make stronger decisions. Through collaborative discussions and arguments, we come up with better ideas." It's about finding skills that are complementary so you can operate efficiently and effectively as a unit. Having that collaborator also allows for work to be streamlined and for more discourse to take place to actually refine the vision as well.

Defining roles helps set clear expectations for what each collaborator is expected to do and accomplish and can make it simple to get things moving. As you lay out and define the roles, recognizing and acknowledging the strengths of each person is important. For a company like Leaf Shave, whose owners are in two different states, this definition of roles has allowed them to work independently together and still see great success. They know their own responsibilities, so while collaboration happens frequently, they are also able to make quick decisions to keep things moving when it falls into their area. "We work independently and touch base once a day. I think that has been good for the business, even though it seems counterintuitive. We get to make decisions quickly, which contributes to our overall success." Quick decision making directly contrasts the idea of unanimity, which can halt progress and interrupt creativity. They are in agreement on the ultimate goal but recognize that there are different pathways to achieving it. "We trust our instincts, and if we don't trust in something that we have created, we won't put it out on the market." When collaborators hit a deadlock and don't have predefined roles, it inhibits the ability to move forward without someone compromising their ideas. A certain level of trust has to exist in order to successfully work together, so predefined roles completely eradicate this issue while still allowing for conversation and the ability to evolve ideas.

DOCUMENTATION
WITH DAN MEDICI

Having always been creative, Dan Medici, a freelance photographer and graphic design editor, had to negotiate the time commitment the arts required once he got to college. He shifted gears from drawing and studied graphic design and marketing in college. While studying formally in classes, Dan was able to continue his own professional development and continued doing freelance photography to supplement his income. This experience of working on your own professional development while studying subjects that can supplement your career is very in line with the ability to collaborate and have more to bring to the table.

"While doing all this freelance work with photography and graphic design, I realized that being in the creative field is what satisfies me and what fulfills my creative appetite," Dan shared. As Dan began wrapping up his college career, he got involved in creating video content with a friend of his, Matt Szczygiel, who was working with country music artists. The pair began working with country music star Luke Combs, and in October they partnered up and made a bid for the Luke Combs Tour. They spent months together prepping their bid and a presentation, and then in mid-January of this year they got the call from Luke Combs' management green-lighting their bid. "We spent a lot of time refining our ideas in order to remain professional because it was our first major contract. We wanted to make sure we put our best foot forward. We spent ten days editing, revising, and coming up with new ideas; we made backup content in case what we had didn't work. You always want to be prepared for other artists who are involved in having adjustments." This is a really interesting part of collaboration when you are bringing something premade to the table: being ready to make adjustments and having backup plans.

"We had to work with other people on the graphics, like the lighting artist, and we had to make sure that all of our work would come together and look good." They were able to fall into their roles and propose new ideas from their background to develop new concepts that would work for the tour. "It was very exciting as a new professional. Luke Combs is at the top of the country music industry, so it added a lot of pressure as well as excitement." Dan had the opportunity to collaborate with lots of professionals for ten days straight as they developed the visuals for the tour.

"We wanted to make sure that we documented everything we were doing and make sure that we didn't do anything without keeping in mind that it has to be a business, and profitable for us."

DAN MEDICI

"Some of the people we were collaborating with worked with big names like Metallica, so it was so exciting when they liked something we made." Their collaboration dealt with many different departments like the video jockey, the lighting designer, and the producers. "We had to be flexible and make things that were easy to work with and easy to adjust when they needed to." That ability to adjust and accommodate feedback with ease instantly adds a more professional touch to your work. Dan was even receiving great feedback from seasoned professionals as a novice in the field.

That ability to be flexible translates into any aspect of life, but something that may be lost on many people is documenting that flexibility. "We wanted to make sure that we documented everything we were doing and make sure that we didn't do anything without keeping in mind that it has to be a business, and profitable for us." Whenever something is going well, you want to document it so you can go back and do it again. If you forget to keep track, you might forget how you did it or how you got there, and that should never happen. When something isn't working, the documentation can help you see where exactly you went wrong and correct it, rather than reinventing the wheel every time.

"Aside from keeping track of how we were creating the graphics, we also needed to document our process and create professional materials to use for promotions. This way we could indicate for people who remember the visuals from that tour that we created them. We have to keep our archives and have our ducks in a row." Documentation is crucial, especially in an environment where you might be making lots of changes and being flexible. This way you can see where you derailed from the original plan and look back on it for future projects. It can also help with marketing yourself to new clients when they ask you about your processes.

"Since that tour, we have been reaching out to other people in the country music world; we are so lucky to have gotten our foot in the door with Luke Combs. Our visuals tied into the meaning of the songs to the point that Luke Combs came up to us and expressed his excitement and gratitude for the visuals and the way they worked out." Coming off the end of a massive project like that and looking into how to move forward, Dan is learning how to create a rapport with his clientele. Networking really comes into play here, and that is where you can use your documentation to your advantage.

"There are so many people who can do the job just as good as you can, but you need to show up and be a good person and be the person that people want to work with." This relies heavily on your ability to market yourself and demonstrate what you have done previously. Having a record of all of your projects and how successful they were will help you to build up a portfolio that you can share with your clients and even use to walk them through the technicalities if needed. "It is a lot about being technically skilled, but also making sure that you are a good person to be around and things like that." Matt and Dan were able to have a successful partnership because they worked out a lot of the business details in the beginning. Documentation doesn't just come into play with clients, but it can be helpful in navigating partnerships as well.

Dan had a great kickstart working on the Luke Combs tour and has successfully documented that process and used it to propel himself forward in his industry. "Going forward, we have been trying to figure out how to step it up and take it to the next level; we are both learning how to use new programs, and we have both looked into where we want to be with our next projects." As freelance creators, they are constantly thinking about the next big step to keep them moving forward with their career. Dan had the chance to discover what he liked doing with the Luke Combs tour production and can now use that understanding to drive his future endeavors.

TAILORING YOUR EDUCATION WITH TAYLOR HENDRI

———

Newborn and wedding photographer Taylor Hendri found that education was a major asset to her professional career and her ability to collaborate. From other photographers' resources to her own formal education, Taylor constantly looks for ways to educate herself and learn new perspectives and skills. This effort to constantly learn, change, adapt, and improve has helped Taylor with different aspects of her professional endeavors, including customer service, promoting her brand, and engaging with her community. As far as collaboration, aside from the obvious collaborations with her clients, Taylor uses her constant education to aid in her collaborative abilities and her overall versatility as an artist and a professional.

"I look to photographers that I look up to and take their courses and advice and learn from them. It's great to have a community where we can use each other as resources." Taylor is able to use her desire to learn as an opportunity to collaborate. You can see the flip side where the collaboration is also an opportunity to learn. Education and collaboration really go hand in hand for the aforementioned parallels. Education is crucial to collaboration because you may need to learn a new skill in order to collaborate, or the collaboration may teach you new skills in an unexpected way.

Taylor shared some of her sentiments with me about the necessary skills to run her business successfully, and something she found was that customer service is imperative. "Anyone can take a good picture, but the service that comes along with it really matters and makes a difference in your business." I think a lot of people can get behind how important customer service is to any business, but it's especially crucial for creative ones where you are tailoring your product to your client. "Something I have been trying to do is to keep educating myself and use resources from other photographers who have made it big in the industry." This ability to continually educate yourself directly relates to what type of services you can offer to your clients. The more you learn, the more of an asset you make yourself to customers and clientele.

Something really interesting Taylor and I discussed was how in her field, both novice photographers and professionals have a lot to learn from each other. "You sometimes have a second shooter or an assistant or associative. There are creative differences, and technology is changing a lot, so there is so much to be learned whether you are a seasoned expert or just starting out." It seems important to acknowledge that all different levels of expertise have something to offer. This is obviously relevant for photographers, but this idea can carry over into lots of different fields and types of work. Give the new guy a chance to share his voice: it can pay off, and it is probably worthwhile. That is how this desire for education looks outside of a formal classroom setting: giving someone the opportunity to share their experience or idea, even though they may not be seasoned.

Taylor described how much the field of photography varies from style to style, which adds to the argument that education can only make you more versatile and useful. "I have been taking pictures since I was fifteen; I became interested in learning different types of photography as I have gone on, and there are so many different kinds of photographers. Studio photography and family photography involve so many different things. Each little niche of the industry is so different. I have dabbled in different types of photography, and I have worked for lots of different places." This understanding of how different types of professionals work has certainly led Taylor to develop her own skills and style while taking tips from lots of different minds along the way. That embodies collaboration in and of itself, but she can also now bring much more to the table because of her collaborations.

Taylor's varied studies in college really led her to success with professional endeavors as well. "I majored in business and HR. While I love and want to do photography, I now have the ability to have a backup plan, fall-back options, and a greater variety in what I can bring to my clients." It's important to keep your options open and make sure you can bring a lot to the table. Taylor recommends taking advantage of the opportunity to double major or studying something that makes you versatile with lots of options. The more skill sets you possess, the easier it is to market yourself. Versatility in your education is an asset that can make you a highly desirable candidate for collaborative projects.

TRANSPARENCY WITH CAPE MAY BREWING COMPANY

In 2011, three men brought their skills together and combined them into something unique. They brewed up an idea for a carry-out local beer, and a decade later, they enjoy the position of being the largest in the state of New Jersey. Ryan Krill, CEO, says they accomplished this feat with their unique perspective and dedication to transparency. Because they put transparency first, they have grown X percent year over year.

Ryan and his team use transparency as a weapon, a tool, and a Magic 8-Ball. If someone makes a mistake, they look to their policy of transparency to guide them. If something goes wrong, they use the idea of transparency to remind them of the right thing to do. The challenges they encounter may seem obvious, but transparency has been an important "North Star" for Ryan and his team.

One collaborative change Ryan shared with me is their shift to open-book management. Essentially, every employee needs to receive training to understand income statements and balance sheets, which then allows all employees to understand the finances of the company. This encourages open communication about what money is going toward and allows for all employees of the business to collaborate and adhere to budgets and own their spending. "I've always been very collaborative in nature; I am very inclusive and like to get peoples input, but this is just a formal way of doing it and a proven system. It makes us organized and thoughtful, and our finances [are] easier to manage."

Ryan also shared that this effort for transparency has eliminated the feeling of being micromanaged for his employees. "I don't pretend like I have all the answers or that I know what I'm doing all the time. We are building this plane—help me fly it." This inverted effort of management and super-transparency helps eliminate any animosity that could develop between different levels of staff and seeing the effects it can have on collaboration is really remarkable.

"The pressure isn't just on me because I am the CEO: it's on everyone equally, the way we structure ourselves. We have full transparency across the board, so we do financial literacy training with all of our employees and understanding the impact of their actions on those documents," Ryan told me in our interview. Those financial documents are sometimes never seen or understood by employees, which can lead to potential issues with the management chain. By encouraging transparency, the employees then get to take ownership in the failures and successes. "We found that our company morale has improved significantly with this transparency effort; I find that people will come to me and own their budgets and will be accountable for them. I am not the decision maker, so they don't need to come to me for every decision; it puts it back on them to own their decisions and own what they have created." This is in some ways really contrary to what we might expect from a company, but its success has been obvious.

Leadership in most businesses is like a triangle with the CEO at the top. Cape May has inverted that triangle and put their front-line folks at the top, while management is at the bottom providing resources to managers, who then provide those to the front-line staff. "My role is to serve them, and they ultimately serve our guests. It's all about service, not being served." Allowing his employees to have a degree of autonomy allows for accountability. "It's about making promises to the company and fulfilling those promises."

Cape May is expanding rapidly. Rapid expansion can sometimes compromise the integrity of core values, but Ryan said this expansion constantly gives them the opportunity to understand who they are and who they are not. "We think critically about this. Why do we get out of bed in the morning? Our purpose is to enjoy the moment, the experience, and beer is an experience, and it's all about pleasure and enjoyment." Knowing what motivates their company to make their product helps drive this rapid expansion and keep it aligned to their values. This transparency effort allows everyone to be on the same page about reaching goals and staying true to their mission.

The remarkable growth they have experienced over the years has also given Ryan and his company the opportunity to reflect

on what has gotten them to where they are. All of these initia-
tives toward transparency and inverted management systems
show that they are not resting on their success, but rather
constantly trying to improve and make their company better.

One of the most powerful things Ryan said to me during
our entire interview was this: "Mistakes are allowed, but no
surprises." I encourage you to take a moment and consider
this, whether you are an employee, a manager, and aspiring
entrepreneur, or an artist. In business, mistakes are so often
criticized and met with anger or demotion. Shifting the narrative around mistakes creates a safe environment for people
to push new ideas. The transparency and support within Cape
May has created an environment where employees can explore
an idea, have access to the materials to see if they can really
make it work, and then go for it. This type of collaboration
can be so powerful for an expanding business, but only if the
fear of negative results isn't looming over employees' heads.
So many people hold back from being creative because they
are afraid of failure. Some people hold back for fear for failure
that may ultimately result in job loss, even. Cape May has
shifted the culture around this and encouraged people to
own their ideas, own their mistakes, and learn from them.
Their mistakes are simply a stepping-stone to being better.
Ryan said that rather than holding those mistakes over their
employees, they empower them to recognize a mistake, talk
about it, and prepare them to deal with those mistakes in the
best way possible to avoid them again in the future.

Transparency can open the door to so much success for a
company, just like it has for Cape May. Many companies
prefer to keep their financial information away from their

employees, mainly for the company's own gain. By giving its employees the resources to understand balance sheets, Cape May has shifted from worrying strictly about capital to caring more for its employees and taking their suggestions to heart. This allows for more collaboration within Cape May, as the company is built on a foundation of trust. Any employee can question any balance sheet; the responsibility of making sure money goes where it needs to falls on many people instead of just a few.

STAYING TRUE TO YOUR MISSION WITH ARTIZANNS

———

In an age where media dominates our daily conversation, narratives and storytelling are wildly important. The ability to control the story of your brand and your business is crucial as you start and continue to grow. If you can identify your story and learn how to tell it with passion and authenticity, others will retell it that way for you. Suzanne Farley shared her sentiments about relaying the passion behind her brand when she shared the story of her gift gallery, Artizanns.

As an involved member in the community in Naples, New York, Suzanne recognized the talent around her and saw that local artists needed a place to display and sell their work. Mass manufacturing and the Amazon-world have compromised the role of the artisan, so she decided to open Artizanns and give local artists the place they needed. "I had a vision of putting together a small gift gallery of local artists' work." It was extremely important to Suzanne to focus on and prioritize the work of local artisans and promoting them: "I didn't want to incorporate the world." With so many businesses trying to create access to goods from all over, Suzanne wanted to focus on giving access to local goods. She wanted to shine a light on her community and the artisans within it.

Internet shopping has grown exponentially, and people don't shop as much in person as they used to. That is why Suzanne stayed true to local artisans only. "Initially, I had thirty-five artists in 2004; that grew to one hundred and twenty-five by 2006." Suzanne credits this incredible growth to her ability to share her story. Naples is a small town, so everyone knows each other. Suzanne knows the people who control the media, and so in that way, she is able to tell her story and allow them to retell it in a way that really gets her passion across to her audience. "I am so passionate about what I am doing, so I have been able to write my own story through the connections I have in the media." This is where the idea of controlling the brand comes in. Having media connections and knowing your market become extremely important. Collaborating with the people who will share your story is not only important, but necessary. Having a good relationship with the media allows for you to work with them to get your story out there in a way that is authentic to your brand.

The fact that some businesses and artists get more press than others is no surprise, but why? Suzanne suggested to me that a lot of this has to do with passion and drive that stems from one's mission. "The reason I got so much great media attention was because of the *passion* I had for the design and use of my gallery. My passion was obvious, and my media connections could recognize that." The great press followed quickly behind the hard work and dedication that was put into the steadfast mission of Artizanns. From day one, it was all about keeping it local and not changing that. While the business grew, it never changed its mission or lost sight of it. This dedication to its mission of keeping local artisans at the forefront allowed for the narrative to be consistent and continuous. After just two years of business, Suzanne outgrew her first space, and as the business changed and experienced growth, she stuck to her initial goal. To this day, Suzanne's shop is teeming with incredible work from artists all over the Finger Lakes region, but that's it. She keeps it local, and she always has. Even with the growth, she never lost sight of her brand, and this is how she has been able to collaborate with the people sharing her story.

"Those personal interactions generate a really intimate customer base that you cannot generate just being online. I have repeat customers from all over the country, and they always make it a point to come here when they visit." Part of the mission Suzanna has been pushing for the years with Artizanns is the need to interact with local artisans, so it makes sense that the internet challenged this sentiment. However, bringing in new owners is allowing for this next step in the evolution of Artizanns to take place. A consistent story and mission can only continue to grow and amass a great reputation. "I didn't think that I could just set up a website and sell stuff. I needed to have a reputation and people backing me. I don't think any social media website would qualify my business the way my solid customer base does. I have years of customer interactions to validate the quality of my store and my products." These customer relationships perpetuate the narrative around her company, too. This is, in a way, a collaboration with her customers.

By creating a great and strong customer base and being consistent in the mission of Artizanns, she gives her customers the tools to promote the business with or without her knowing. When you eat at a great restaurant, you tell people. When you find a great shop, you recommend it to your friends. Giving businesses good press is a sort of indirect collaboration. On the flip side, negative experiences deter you, and inconsistent businesses often deter people as well. "I have developed this one-on-one relationship with my customers, and to me that is the most valuable promotion you could ever have: working one-on-one with your customers—they are the way to generating more customers." Because of these incredible customer interactions, Artizanns has been a huge success.

Now, with over two hundred artisans, Artizanns has continued to represent the community of artists in the local area. Suzanne discussed how over the course of opening her business, she has seen the growth of different platforms for marketing and sales, the most obvious being e-commerce options. Suzanne recognized that while the internet had many advantages, in some ways it would take away from an aspect of her business that was important to her. "I wanted to bring people in to see, touch, and feel this amazing work that I have in this amazing building. I kept fighting the internet, but I think that young people don't necessarily have the time to 'shop' like they used to." Suzanne has been growing with her business, and she has begun to recognize the value e-commerce would bring to her little shop. This is why the decision to sell her business was not easy.

"I am really proud of what I created."

SUZANNE FARLEY

Suzanne is planning to retire, and she has gladly found just the right people to take over Artizanns. "It has been a real comfortable road of passionate success with everything I have done and developed: sixteen years of business, and I am really proud of what I created." She has spent the past sixteen years creating an amazing brand and stayed true to it. She is now working with the new owners to "phase them in" and help them understand what Artizanns is all about. They are bringing that New-Age touch and have plans for e-commerce that will bring Artizanns into its next phase. As she collaborates with the new owners, one thing she will share with them is her mission to keep it local. They have great excitement to grow with the business and build off of the amazing reputation Suzanne has made for the shop.

CREATING A BRAND WITH SERINA CHUGANI AND SAMMY NAPOLITANO

———

Friends of eight years Serina and Sammy took their unconventional creativity and "not-so-chill" attitudes to create a brand that is completely representative of women's empowerment and that breathes collaboration. I had the pleasure of interviewing Serina and Sammy together, and their passion and energy was so obvious as we got into the driving factor behind their new company: female empowerment. During the COVID-19 pandemic, the girls decided to capitalize on their time in quarantine, and Not So Chill Girls was born. "We are both 'not so chill' girls and believe in women's empowerment: 'chill girls only' is not the only way! Women prescribe to this idea of being chill to be valued by men, and we are taking control of that label and telling them not to be chill and instead being unapologetically themselves," Serina shared. With the younger generation, the word "chill," meaning "relaxed" and "go-with-the-flow," is thrown around a lot. There is definitely a narrative that "chill girls" are the ones you want to be around. Sammy and Serina are channeling their passion for fashion and using it as a way to combat this narrative.

Sammy remarked, "When we were originally brainstorming this idea, it came up because someone once said I was the least chill girl she knew...Why? Because I'm outspoken and have strong opinions and ambition. So a major part of ambition is helping others. It's hard to articulate, but having a bigger message goes along with it being more than just clothes—outspoken and ambitious, standing up for what we believe in, and being empowered in what we're wearing. It was coming at a time during COVID and BLM all came up, and as we were gaining more traction [we asked], 'How can we incorporate others into our business?'"

"A lot of the things that are the opposite of being chill are what make you a boss lady," Sammy said. She feels that when women share their goals, achievements, and ambitions, it appears as bragging in some way. Now, both young professionals and entrepreneurs, Sammy and Serina realized that "not being chill" is exactly what empowered them to dive right in. Sammy does a lot of the paperwork, and once they started bouncing the idea around, she took the initiative to file for their LLC. "I genuinely enjoy the work; we filed for our LLC and got our licensing within thirty-six hours." The drive that yielded a thirty-six-hour turnaround for these entrepreneurs is the same drive their brand is encouraging and promoting. Serena shared that starting this business was all about "learning as we go, but knowing that we really believe in this idea, and the message is more important than the daunting task of starting a business." If you have a passion, the brand follows. The pair felt so strongly about this mission that their branding came easily.

We already discussed actions like defining roles and staying organized. Sammy and Serina naturally fell into their roles, which allowed them each to blossom. Serina focuses on defining the mission and the goals, whereas Sammy implements them. "We are so different, so yin and yang, but we are also the same in a lot of ways. It has gone so well, and we can fill in for each other's gaps; we are in this together. If we had started this alone, it would be less about girls standing together." Their brand naturally needed women founders. The key to their whole vision and mission that I think is really important to highlight here is that it is all extremely authentic to them. Their branding isn't forced or fake: it is transparent and true. I know Sammy really well; we actually lived together for a few months in Italy. I can personally attest to her ambition and drive—those "not-so-chill" characteristics they are reclaiming and reframing through their brand.

The pair really complement each other in a way that they want to highlight women should be doing for one another anyway...Serina is learning the back end and logistics from Sammy as they progress. On the flip side, Serina is teaching Sammy about reaching a wider audience and expounding creativity. They are bringing their strengths to the table and offering them to one another—a perfect example of collaboration. "When we are ordering our clothes, we both select a lot of options; Serina sends me things to look at, and we have to compromise on some of our ideas, but everything sells! We are both bringing our styles and merging them together." This business in its very nature is so honest to what the brand stands for that the girls represent their brand without even trying. While conscious decisions about marketing and branding must be made, their support for one another and their "not-so-chill" attitudes really market themselves.

"Isn't our job as women to build each other up and encourage each other?" Serina remarked. "I feel like my place in society right now is really important, and that is to start a brand that stands for something. How can we encourage women to do what they love, be themselves, and focus on what's important in the world?" They are asking big questions and channeling their passions into the answers. "We talked a lot right before we were launching about what our mission was and what we were supporting, and we have faith that what we are putting out there is for us and for the betterment of women, and that's what gets me through."

Sammy added, "Serina pushes me to be outside of my comfort zone with what we are talking about because I tend to focus on the business end and the numbers. The balance with me and Serina is so important because we can be a for-profit business without compromising our mission." Embodying your brand is the best way to create it, and that is exactly what Serina and Sammy have done and are doing.

HONESTY IN COLLABORATION WITH DANIEL DISMUKE

———

What started as a creative conversation with a friend turned into a massive change of direction for filmmaker and author Daniel Dismuke. He and his friend were discussing how they could make a horror thriller trilogy and keep it low budget, and they then took the initiative to turn that conversation into a reality. "I had never worked in writing or film before, but I loved movies growing up. After that conversation, I stuck with it." Daniel began outlining the plot and identifying who the characters were and how it would end. In five months, he wrote *Peter*, and has since published *Peter II*. Daniel credits his success to his honest collaboration efforts and having a transparent creative process.

Having never worked in writing or film, Daniel took his love of movies growing up and began to outline his story. "I started at the end and worked backward. I was filling holes instead of creating all-new things, and that is way easier than starting from scratch. It took me five months in college to write the book, and I changed my major; I knew starting with a book would give me credibility." I think noting that Daniel decided to drop out of school to pursue his book entirely is important. "All I was doing was writing *Peter*, and [I] started focusing all my time on finishing the book, composing a script, and then making it a twenty-page short. I moved home and worked a tech job to get the money to pay for it." No one has suggested that you need to drop out of college to pursue what interests you; I certainly did not. But what you can take away from this is that it is worth *considering* if the investment in college will ultimately serve you. Daniel shared how important being honest with himself has been throughout his entire story, and it starts with really evaluating whether or not various choices are really serving you and the ending you want to meet.

"Collaboration was at the center of my film. That collaboration was reliant on honesty between me and everyone I worked with." Transparency and honesty are such crucial parts of successful collaboration—and not just in the film industry. Building a relationship with your partners, clients, and yourself is so useful to establish a standard for how your collaboration will go. Daniel knew he was just getting started in the industry, and the only way to learn and make waves was by finding others who needed that same shot. He was up-front about what he was trying to accomplish but also steadfast in his work toward making it a success. After Daniel saw how successful this approach to collaboration was and how it led to his first film running really smoothly, he decided, "It guides how I handle all my new projects."

So what is the secret? Why am I even talking about how important honesty is? I think people generally understand that being honest is important, but maybe don't know exactly what "honesty" looks like in regard to collaboration. For Daniel, "It is all about not having too much ego and being honest about what is happening. When someone comes up to you and suggests that something might work better, listen to their suggestions. I have learned to drop my ego and branch out into more successful collaboration." Collaboration is all about combining ideas: even if the project is ultimately yours, you can use honesty to your advantage. Being up-front about every aspect of the project is crucial. This honest nature extends to really defining what your expectations are but not being overly attached to them. You know where you want to go, but are you open to different ways of getting there?

Daniel is living in San Diego, California, and working on more projects that include honest collaboration. He talked about how learning how to work with other people makes you more well-rounded and gives you an opportunity to gain new experiences that you couldn't have in other ways. "*Peter* had a lot going on; we had to adjust and change things. Now, a lot of the projects I am working on are simpler in comparison because I have already learned how to honestly and collaboratively finish a project." Daniel just released *Peter II* this year and is spending a lot of time working on short films. These short film projects have given Daniel the opportunity to open up and explore new avenues of communication with different producers. He stressed how taking his time and being honest and realistic has allowed him to explore different worlds in his industry. Collaboration and getting used to working with other people give you successful assets and the opportunities to gain experience.

This idea of unfiltered honesty is also really important when it comes to how you work with yourself. Instead of being discouraged, Daniel keeps himself motivated by constantly allowing himself to know his capabilities. "Part of it is just knowing what I'm capable of and that I've gotten to learn and absorb so much information through my experiences, and I trust myself and I am amazed by what I have accomplished. I also know there is a lot more to learn." This honesty really goes hand in hand with successful collaboration. "It's about being honest with yourself and knowing what you are capable of, and then looking to people who are successful and seeing what you can learn from them." Being honest with yourself can sometimes be the biggest challenge of all, but it leads to a really positive mindset.

MIXING IT UP WITH
REMIX FITNESS

———

Tricia Goodman, one of two founders of Remix Fitness, has an amazing philosophy that not only guides her business, but is also extremely important in collaboration: mix it up! Tricia and her partner, Mary Kate, met when they were teaching at a small boutique fitness studio. They loved that small intimate feeling but felt a bit bored by the lack of variety. Mary Kate approached Tricia with the idea of creating a similar boutique but having lots of options for workouts. They dove into the project, and in just over a year, Remix Fitness was created. They pulled advice and guidance from their connections and had an executive from Equinox Group, an interior designer, two lawyers, and a commercial real estate agent all helping get their vision together. "The whole concept is to mix it up: you can't do the same thing over and over again." The variety lends itself to a more diverse community but also increases motivation and doesn't allow you to fall into a mundane routine. There is always something new to try, which creates a certain degree of accountability.

"The whole concept is to mix it up: you can't do the same thing over and over again."

TRICIA GOODMAN

After hearing this from Tricia, I decided to look up the benefits of mixing up your routine. I found an article that explained seven reasons why mixing up your fitness routine is good for you.

1. It helps with weight loss. If you are doing the same thing, your body gets used to it, and you burn fewer calories. Making your body constantly adjust to change is good to keep burning the maximum amount of calories.

2. Mixing it up prevents overuse injuries. Instead of using the same muscles over and over, they all get their time to shine and their time to rest.

3. The more you change up the routine, the more all your different muscles get strengthened.

4. Mixing it up keeps you from falling into the same routine and getting bored.

5. It keeps your brain healthy. Mixing it up is good for your brain, and the more you change the routine, the more work your brain does—exercising the mind and body!

6. Mixing it up is good for your social life...You will meet more people in different classes and have a bigger network.

7. Mixing it up keeps things new and exciting.[18]

Now let's look at those same seven reasons and apply them not just to fitness, but also to general collaborative success.

1. Weight loss. Mixing it up and collaborating might allow you to save money, save time, cut down on unnecessary things, etc.

2. Prevents overuse injuries. Mixing it up and collaborating will keep you from burning out, getting exhausted, or potentially losing your passion.

3. Mixing it up and collaborating will allow you to strengthen your abilities in lots of different ways, because with collaboration you can learn so much from others and learn new ways to do things.

4. Mixing it up and collaborating is exciting! Collaborations can bring in so many new ideas and exciting things to break up the monotony of any job or endeavor.

5. It keeps your brain healthy. Mixing it up and collaborating, much the same as exercise, breaks that routine that your brain instinctively knows and forces it to try something new. This is exercising your brain.

---

18   Sally Wadyka, "7 Reasons to Switch Up Your Workout," One Medical, December 7, 2018, https://www.onemedical.com/blog/live-well/7-reasons-to-switch-up-your-workout.

6. Mixing it up and collaborating gives you the chance to meet new partners, clients, and expand your network and outreach.

7. Mixing it up and collaborating can bring just the right amount of energy and excitement back into something that needs a little revival.

This idea of mixing it up and collaborating may feel quite radical to those people who live and die by their routine, but think of this: You can keep doing what you like, but what if you might like something else, too? Or even *more...*? If you think of your innovation the way that Tricia and Mary Kate think of the human body, you can see how beneficial this concept is. "I knew from my personal training background that doing the same things over and over makes your body adapt and plateau, and you have to change it up to see benefits and maintain results. You have to keep challenging your muscles in order for them to improve."

If we treat our creations like we treat our body, we can keep seeing improvement and results. This can manifest in many different ways depending upon what we type of work we are talking about. Are you an artist? Try a new painting technique. If you're used to oils, have you thought of pastels? You're an engineer? Experiment with that new material that you have heard about. You own a business? What other businesses share a common mission that you can collaborate with to expand your customer base? These are just three quick examples. But do you see the power in change? Mixing it up can keep your business on a constant upward trend, just like your body.

"It started when we were working at another other studio and we were doing the same things over and over. Mentally, it's nice to mix it up and try something different." For Remix, one way they collaborate is by having a varied clientele, from kids home from school all the way up to people about seventy years old. "It's really awesome to see in class, having all different levels and ages and everyone feels comfortable coming in no matter what age you are." Their mix of classes and workout routines is a collaboration of fitness styles, which draws in that mixed clientele. Their business is a unique collaboration of fitness and lifestyle ideas that has really paid off. "Collaborating has been the biggest reason why we have been successful." Their unique boutique fitness studio is like none other, and I can personally attest to this, as I have taken a few classes there myself! The ability to constantly welcome change and mix things up really lends itself to successful collaboration.

PART THREE

TESTIMONIES AND STORIES OF COLLABORATIVE SUCCESS

INDIRECT COLLABORATION WITH GROUND LEVEL UP

After attempting to study film and media in a formal setting in London, Carrick McLelland realized it went against the way he liked to learn, and he went on his way back to Scotland and back to square one. "Going to London was this make-it-or-break-it moment," and while it may not have appeared like a "make-it" moment at the time, that "failure" at formal education inspired Carrick to start his company, Ground Level Up, by himself at eighteen years old. "In order to start the company, I had to take out a bank loan, write my business plan, get a website, establish a brand, and buy all of my equipment." That first big step in making his company come to life has a lot to do with his ability to take inspiration from other companies and adopt it to his own vision and mission. This way of collaborating is inspiration-based and indirect. Carrick mastered this when he was establishing himself as a young professional, and that ability to harness indirect collaboration led him to great success just a few short years down the road.

When you are really young, it can be challenging to get people to take you seriously. Carrick was no stranger to this, and he shared that "Trying to get myself taken seriously for people to want to pay for my services was my biggest challenge." What is the best way to work around this? Whether you are young or just inexperienced in whatever field you have decided to enter, there is an opportunity when you have people who inspire you who are doing similar work. This is where that indirect collaboration really comes into play. By adopting ideas from other companies and seeing what they look like within your own practice, you have found a way to "collaborate" without having to actually work with anyone but yourself.

Carrick found that this method really helped him get off the ground in the beginning. "If you are taking inspiration from a company that's been around longer than you, and you apply their methods and styles to your projects, you have essentially collaborated with that company in a roundabout way." That is where Carrick began with collaboration. This may seem a bit strange, given that the idea behind collaboration is to work together, but think of it in this way: when you really admire something someone has done, you model yourself after them, but you find ways to make it your own. "I was extremely active in terms of seeing what's out there and seeing what the companies I felt inspired by did and then experimenting with how that could work for me. That's how you can collaborate without any connections. I looked at who I was impressed by and figured out how to make it my own." There is an opportunity to take inspiration and adopt it into your own practices. It really has to do with this philosophy that there is nothing new—just new ways of executing the same things. Carrick didn't invent anything, he revolutionized it: in the same way that the goal of this book is to look into the possibility of reviving Italian Renaissance ideas, Carrick revived other professionals' ideas and added his personal take.

The journey Carrick has had with collaboration is really important for young people and novices because not everyone has connections to big names or the resources to build up a big team. "I was a one-man program, and so collaborating with an actual team was difficult because I didn't have the budget." Carrick found success by working with whoever he wanted to, even if he didn't hire them. That sounds confusing, right? This is how he did it: "If you want to work with someone, you have to go and do it. That is how you show that you want to work with a client. Go to the store and buy their product, do a shoot, reach out with your work, and show them what you've done. This is how you prove yourself. This worked for Ground Level Up, and you can apply that to anything, not just photography. When I reached out to the clients I wanted, I actually had something to show them." Whether or not Carrick was getting those big contracts, he was building up his portfolio, which then gave him something to show for his work.

Slowly, he started getting clients. Eventually he was getting contracts with the types of brands and clientele he wanted. "It can get frustrating in the beginning, but if you are young or just starting out, your work won't sell itself: you can't just sit back and wait for clients to show up; you have to market yourself." This idea of indirect collaborations is really powerful. It serves the purpose, firstly, of doing the work you are passionate about, and, secondly, building up work to show potential clients.

"Once I had established myself, my work did begin to sell itself."

CARRICK MCLELLAND

Complacency and passion don't mix, and Carrick articulates this so well. He didn't let any boundaries prevent him from creating the work he wanted to create. He was all in on his business, dedicating himself to it full time. "If you are really passionate about what you want to do, you will be doing it regardless of the profit, so start doing the work that you want to do and use that to build your portfolio and your reputation." All of a sudden, those collaborations that are one-sided will evolve into in-person collaborations with the clients and partners you want. "I had to prove myself first to a lot of my clients to get them to engage with me. I had to do a lot of work for cheap, but I also had to understand that a lot of the companies could have worked with a different company with more of a reputation than I had; I had to build my experience base-up. Then, once I had established myself, my work *did* begin to sell itself." That is what has gotten Carrick and Ground Level Up to where they are at now, and this is where a more traditional notion of collaboration really came in.

As Carrick began to get himself a professional reputation, his business began to expand. All of a sudden, he felt at odds with two directions to go in: continue on his own and raise his prices or be in a team and relinquish some of the control over the work. "When you are an artist in this industry, you have two options: contain full control of your work and be the sole artist behind your brand, or you can turn it into a company and a commercial vibe and be able to do things on a bigger scale. I could either begin to raise my prices and [have] people paid to work with only me, or I could bring in more people and develop a company with a reputation." This crossroads that Carrick faced happens in all sorts of situations, not just in media. As a company or project grows and expands, something has to give. Carrick chose the latter of the two...

Carrick decided finding people he really trusted was best for his company. "I give them the agency to deliver the product in the name of the company, even if it wasn't my hands creating the product. I had to release some control." This can be something challenging to shift into when the collaboration goes from one-sided to more traditional. "I had a way that I did things, but in order to grow my business to the scale I wanted, I needed other people—but in doing so I had to accept that it wasn't always my way. Having employees that I trust because I believe that they are delivering quality content to my clients was extremely important in the process of giving up some of that control."

Ground Level Up is now an extremely successful company with multiple employees that prides itself on inexpensive, high quality, and quickly produced media. They are continuing to grow exponentially and ultimately looking at mass video production capabilities. They are working out how much capacity they can handle and preparing to roll out their massively scaled production in the near future. Carrick and his team are even considering launching an idea that will educate staff at other companies on how to make their own content in-house. All of these amazing opportunities became possible with one young man, seeing who was doing it right, and engaging in one-sided collaboration.

LEADING BY EXAMPLE WITH LIFE'S GOJI

———

Leadership is inherently collaborative: a leader is not a leader without their followers. In Somers Point, New Jersey, local couple Scott and Julia harnessed their passions by opening their juice bar, Life's Goji. "Goji started because Scott and I always wanted to help the greater good and to open a restaurant because we are passionate about food," says Julia. "We know how important it is to build up the community, and so when we had the opportunity to take over a brand that we identified with, and it met our needs, we went for it. It is health-based and all about bringing healthy food to people of all income levels, it's sustainable, and when the opportunity presented itself to us, we realized this is it. It is a passion project and it felt right."

Scott and Julia shared a passion for food and it only seemed natural that a restaurant would allow them to combine their passions into a project that encompassed it all. They opened Goji in 2019, and Julia has described their operations as a "sprint" because they were met with crazy support and success within their community. From the day their doors opened, business was booming in a way they had never anticipated. The demand for their business has not slowed down to this day. The lens through which Scott and Julia have viewed their role as business owners is a really unique way to look at collaboration as well as their personal responsibility for promoting the greater good with their business. Leadership is inherently collaborative, as you cannot be a leader without your followers.

Goji was previously started as a juice bar by another couple, and Scott and Julia took it over and expanded it in 2019. They opened up a storefront and took the brand to the next level. "It has been a big learning curve opening up and finding ourselves in a space where we need to identify what is the 'greater good' and how can we get that to the people. We want to do the most responsible things and not worry about what other businesses are doing. We want to be leaders." Their mission to serve their community and the greater good is brought about in their five values: use real, healthful ingredients, keep it affordable, reduce waste, buy local, and always be fresh. For Scott and Julia, the greater good of caring for the human body and the planet that collectively houses us all is best served by adhering to these five values. Having clear and definable values has allowed them to make sure that their decisions align to their ultimate vision as well as set up clear standards for the example they wish to set in their community.

I find Scott and Julia's story so interesting because that initial takeover of the brand was extremely collaborative. They didn't start from scratch: they adopted someone else's existing brand

and took it to a new place. The foundations of Goji already existed from the previous owners, Scott and Julia took parts of that original vision and then modified and expanded it to become their own. In just this one story, we can recognize how so many different types and scales of collaboration come into play in just one business.

Scott and Julia recognized the social responsibility that comes with opening a business and embraced it head on. By recognizing the social responsibility that came into play as they opened their doors, they entered into a social contract with their customers and community. This is a new way of doing business; embracing this collaborative leadership can really enhance the relationship with your customers.

Scott and Julia were collaborating with the community just by making their products affordable, accessible, and locally sourced. "Our biggest thing is making this type of product accessible and finding ways that we can offer our customers their favorite foods and flavors but in healthy options and meeting people in their lifestyles now. We are not trying to change people's lives but advocating that they need to try and make better choices for themselves." I love how relevant this idea is: the way they are collaborating is by simply existing.

Think about your lifestyle. Perhaps you are not physically active (I'm not nearly as much as I should be), but you have a friend who is fit and always hitting the gym,. They are constantly judging you for your lack of exercise, telling you that you need to do it more, trying to *force* that lifestyle on you. You probably aren't going to respond well and may even now have a worse connotation with working out than you did to begin with! Now look at the method Scott and Julia are using: they eat healthy, they make it tasty and affordable, and they don't force anyone in the doors or judge the people who haven't embraced their lifestyle. They simply exist with open arms and share their positive results and passion. *THIS* is much more effective. Just by being open and promoting certain lifestyle choices, they encourage people to adopt them themselves. For example, they have a reusable bottle system, so if you buy a juice it comes in a glass jar, and when you bring it back to refill, you get a discount and you're making a more eco-friendly and health-conscious choice. It's positive reinforcement, *and* it encourages healthy, sustainable choices.

As I described before, Scott and Julia's system is a community collaboration to create a healthier, more sustainable community. In order for something to be sustainable, there must be a group of people who sustain it, and in this case, Life's Goji and their customers are working together and sharing that common goal. "We work together and work to our strengths. I come up with lots of ideas, and then Scott and I find ways to make them happen by building up the community. We feature local artists every few months and try to keep everything, including our products, local." The very act of adhering to their values shows they are on the right path and on an upward trend. Even during the COVID-19 pandemic, they worked extremely hard to offer their products to their clients in a safe, healthy, and sustainable way.

Scott and Julia have exemplified how collaboration can be subtle but powerful and how leading by example is extremely collaborative. Leaders must have followers, and without them, they are not leaders. One cannot exist without the other.

Followers learn from, emulate, and take after their leaders, and in the same light, leaders adjust their processes to accommodate and better serve their followers. Scott and Julia constantly adapt their offerings, listen to their customers, and adhere to their values, demonstrating this collaborative leadership. In the last chapter, Carrick talked about how he looked up to certain professionals and adopted their philosophies and ideas to better himself. Although they are in a different industry, Scott and Julia are the type of professionals people look up to and collaborate with indirectly. "At the end of the day, we want to help people, be compassionate, and give people the chance to do what they are the best at doing: being their best, healthiest selves."

LARGE AND SMALL-SCALE COLLABORATIONS WITH PETER VERGARA AND DR. TOM FLAHERTY

———

Peter Vergara of Sotheby's auction house handles some of the most high-end collaborations in the fine art world. He told me, "I think collaboration is equally as broad as the art world itself." Within the art market, of lot of the day-to-day activity relies on art history. Peter began his career with art history the same way many of us have, in AP Art History. Peter and I went to high school together, and we both had our interest in the field piqued by the same teacher, Mrs. Micheletti. "Those years of formative education have the opportunity to ignite passion within students, but only if the teacher really knows how to include collaboration within the classroom." Our experience wasn't just monotonous lectures: it included engaging discussions, relevant films, challenging visual analyses, and an opportunity for a "living art show."

"I think collaboration is equally as broad as the art world itself."

PETER VERGARA

Education is extremely powerful, and the ability to integrate these ideas into the classroom only adds value to learning opportunities. Peter first found his initial interest in the field during high school; he then led internships at museums during college, and now he works at Sotheby's promoting collaborative experiences. It's fascinating how experiences from so long ago can continue to impact us well into our adult lives and careers—I think that speaks to the importance of educators in our lives. I know Peter and I both are grateful to Mrs. Micheletti for taking the time to engage us in the world of art history.

As we shift gears to really dive into Peter's role in the auction world, it's important to recognize that this is one facet of the "art world" that has a lot more in common with big business than local artisans. For example, Christie's, Sotheby's, and other major auction houses are internationally recognized companies that have massive networks and roots that date as far back as the 1700s. As you read about Peter's experience and work at Sotheby's, keep in mind that the business has been around for as long as much of the art it is auctioning off. "Collaboration in this setting is very formal and corporate, but there is also a very social aspect to the art world with dealers and artists. The world of art in that sense is very small, and everyone knows each other." The larger your operation gets, the more formal and corporate the collaboration is going to be.

While this is pretty different from most of the stories we have encountered this far, we need to recognize that creative collaboration has no limits. It can continue and extend even within the biggest operations. "The auction world innately breathes communication and collaboration because it's a small world, despite how big the companies are. I don't know what this would look like in finance or banking, but in this world, you develop a network very quickly, and so as a result the auction house world itself is a big collaboration." Sotheby's operates as one of the largest auction houses in existence and constantly has work coming in and out of its doors all over the world. When a work of art comes to Sotheby's, preparations begin and require a host of people. Peter is just one part of this massive collaborative puzzle. This speaks to the idea of credit as well as the unseen hands that we have touched on previously in the book.

It all starts with the excited seller, looking for someone with the means to sell it—that's where Sotheby's comes in. Sotheby's has the stage and the market. Any person who has a collection would contact an auction house to help them with the sale. These auction houses are a great way to get the right eyes on an object and bring in the highest price tag.

"Before anyone can even get their hands on the work, there are a myriad of different teams that come into play." Operations, who move the work, are literally in charge of the physical movement from point A to point B. They help collect the work from the seller and bring it to the auction house safely and in one piece.

Then we move on to the legal team. This team is extremely important, especially when we are talking about a company that deals with international sales. This team is well versed on the laws that govern the sale, how these laws change from country to country, and any legal paperwork and documentation that must be provided.

The marketing team is very important for public sales, and it works closely with the cataloging team, which documents and researches the work. The catalogue gives buyers an opportunity to browse prior to a public sale, and the marketing team uses this catalogue to boost interest around the works being sold and bring in more buyers.

Depending on the type of work or object, more or fewer people need to get involved, but according to Peter, "It really takes a village to coordinate a sale of any given work, let alone a sale with three hundred items. What really drives collaboration in our business is getting artwork on that world stage and in the exhibition spaces. It's about putting on an auction that gives the works new life, a new spotlight, and ultimately a new home. *That* takes a village."

This massive collaboration is much different from the ways we have already engaged with collaboration, but the scale and the logistics really speak to an aspect of collaboration that can translate into other fields as well. The role Peter plays in this village is handling a lot of those logistics and ultimately bringing the moving parts together.

Before a sale, Peter shared how coordinating an exhibition is a major part of the process. "I don't execute any of those roles specifically, but I help oversee the status of the work as it is in the process of going to auction; I take care of a lot of logistics." For about two weeks leading up to any exhibition, an entire other team comes in that handles the lighting, hanging, shipping, and designing of the exhibition. Artwork is so unique because the artist intended for works to be viewed or engaged with in very specific ways. When curating an exhibition, there is even an aspect of collaboration with the original artist of the work, even if they have long since passed away, because there is an intention to display the work in the way the artist designed, created, and intended it to be seen. Think of something like a stained-glass window: it is very important to view it with light coming through as it would have been *in situ*. If an exhibition is being curated for stained glass, the manner in which the art is displayed would be all about the position of lights, in contrast to perhaps a furniture show, where the objects need to be seen in more utilitarian settings. All of this goes into consideration before planning can even begin. "Setting up an exhibition is in many ways the most collaborative effort, but there are some decisions that are left to one person—the curator."

With a team this massive all working together on different aspects of a sale, there is potential for over-collaborating, which can actually deter the entire process and ultimately slow it down. In a large-scale collaboration such as this, it is absolutely crucial to have a clear hierarchy of decision making and designation of responsibilities. Because artwork is so unique and designing these shows is so intricate, a plethora of ideas may be constantly flowing. At some point, there needs to be a cutoff to begin execution. "Everyone brings different experiences and talents to the table, and since every work has different needs, it can sometimes feel like everyone is fighting to support the needs of their area of expertise." When you have strict timelines and objectives, it is imperative to prioritize the main goal: selling the artwork. Using the tools we learned from Part Two will assist with massive collaborations, because sound decisions can be made quickly with defined roles and clear expectations, among other things. "It's important to hear everyone out, but when you don't have a ton of time to get something together, there has to be an authority figure to make the final call."

DR. TOM FLAHERTY

A service trip to France through his high school led two-time Emmy-winning medical producer Tom Flaherty to pursue his MD. Even though both of his grandfathers were doctors, his first trip to Lourdes was what really got Tom thinking about his potential career as a doctor. He headed to Edinburgh, Scotland and studied history in his first year; when he realized the UK school system couldn't really support his interest in medicine, he transferred to the US and went to Brown University. After fulfilling the premed requirements, Tom coincidentally met a woman who told him about a medicine program for humanities majors, which he applied and was accepted to. That program was at Mount Sinai Hospital in New York, and after four years of hard work, Tom became Dr. Tom. Med school really pushed him, so instead of going into residency, Dr. Tom took a position on *The Dr. Oz Show*, and that's where his experience with collaboration really began.

If you aren't familiar with *The Dr. Oz Show*, it's an American daytime television talk show in which Dr. Oz hosts conversations about health, wellness, and various medical information. He sometimes brings on celebrities or pop-culture references.

Dr. Tom was a writer on this show, and he made sure the information on the show was always medically accurate and fact-checked the scripts. "I graduated as a doctor and got a working visa, and then halfway through my first year they asked me to write and produce a segment for the show."

When Dr. Tom got involved writing his own segment, he had to get creative. It was a big opportunity for him, and an exciting one at that. "I was in charge of animation, and then they asked me to write and produce a segment. It was about a joint disorder that a lot of people suffer from, and so I got a performer from Cirque du Soleil who has a big act where he pulls things with his jaw. That segment was a huge success, so then they asked me to stay on as a producer and a writer." Tom actually left *The Dr. Oz Show* to go and complete his residency, but he regretted leaving such a creative job. "I got back in touch with Dr. Oz, and he invited me back for two years as writer and producer." Dr. Tom went on to win two Emmys for his work on *The Dr. Oz Show*, which is such an amazing accomplishment.

While he felt like collaboration played a huge role in his time at *The Dr. Oz Show*, it's his current position where he really embraced the collaborative practice. "In Costa Rica I met a lovely lady in a supermarket, and her husband and I got to know each other, and her brother is a cofounder for a medical 3D visualization company—and they offered me a job as a medical director there." As medical director, Dr. Tom has been working on lots of projects. One that caught my eye are these one-minute talks with Dr. Tom that explain common health scenarios. Dr. Tom even made one about the coronavirus, which is super relevant right now. "The company I work for now is awesome, and my role is promoting how people can use our company's content, so I make sure the software we have is medically accurate and liaise within our department to our clients and other departments." Having come from *The Dr. Oz Show*, which was a massive production, and moving into a smaller company, Dr. Tom saw a lot of differences right off the bat. "We work for a small company with about forty employees, and we all know each other. We have a really different work environment than *The Dr. Oz Show*." The bigger the production and the more employees that are involved can affect how collaboration works in a very big way.

"I can physically walk to someone's desk to have a chat and collaborate with them, whereas on *Dr. Oz*, collaboration was necessary but was sometimes more difficult. Here, people just offer their collaboration, and we have had an epic result. On *The Dr. Oz Show* roles were more defined, so the nature of collaboration was more rigid, whereas in a smaller environment it can be more off the cuff." In both settings, collaboration is extremely important; it just looks different because of the scale of the operations. "My whole job is collaborative, and it always has been." What is unique about smaller-scale operations is that opportunity to individually get to know the team and understand their strengths. In large-scale collaborative settings, voices and ideas can get lost in the mix, so it's important to set yourself apart. By shifting from a large to a small scale, Dr. Tom saw a major opportunity to engage his team members in multiple projects.

"Sometimes our collaboration is just about availability; other times you play people to their strengths. We have a lot of anatomy projects, and we have one gentleman who is really good at illustrating veins and arteries. Someone else is better at cellular and molecular scenes. It's about recognizing strengths and being aware of availability." Big or small scale, collaborating is made easier when you are around good people who have the skills to collaborate. "With a strong team, the whole collaboration thing comes so naturally, but if you are with a team that lacks cohesion, you don't easily collaborate."

There are obvious pros and cons to both micro and macro collaborations. On a large scale, you have very systematic collaborations and routines for how they work and look. On a smaller scale, it is easier to adapt, make changes, and play to the strengths of every single team member. "Communication is extremely important when collaborating, which I have felt in both roles." Some aspects of collaboration are steadfast, while others need to shift to the dynamics of your team and the size of your team.

COLLABORATION FOR INTROVERTS WITH AMY VOLOSHIN

Having graduated from Rhode Island School of Design and going on to design for Urban Outfitters, Free People, and later start her own textile design firm, Amy Voloshin is not short on impressive accomplishments and entrepreneurial success. I've known Amy for a few years now, and I even interned at her company, Print Fresh, for a summer, so it was natural to reach out to her for an interview about creative collaboration. What surprised me was that Amy said she is quite introverted, and collaboration does not come so naturally to her. I began to wonder how someone featured in *The New York Times Magazine*, *The Philadelphia Inquirer*, and *Forbes*, among others, could be an introvert. Amy was named Young Entrepreneur of the Year by the Philadelphia Chamber of Commerce and was also the recipient of the Arts and Business Council For-Profit Business of the Year. So everyone knows the typical outgoing business person who can talk the talk, that might be a stereotype, but I found learning how Amy has balanced her introverted nature with the creative industry she is in.

In the last four years, Amy has launched her own clothing line, Voloshin, and has shifted the Print Fresh company into the apparel field. To someone like myself, who is constantly chatting and looking for someone to bounce ideas off of, I expected Amy to come right off the bat with all these wonderful stories about how collaboration was the key to her success. What I found, and had failed to consider, is that not everyone is an extrovert who collaboration comes naturally to. "Collaboration is very interesting for me, because when I told [my husband] Leo I was going to be talking to you about collaboration, he kind of laughed. I collaborate in a way that I may not naturally define as collaboration. My process tends to be more isolated. Because I tend to work on deeply creative pieces of design, I sometimes get overwhelmed if I am around a lot of people." This was not at all the answer I was expecting, but it occurred to me when I reflected on our interview that I am writing about how collaboration is extremely flexible and can shift and look different for everyone.

"Sometimes being in a group can be a lot for me. A lot of people in our team work on the pajama brand together, and in that particular group, because a lot of us are quiet and mostly females, we sort of prepare our time together differently." Collaboration is still happening, but it's in a much different way from a lot of the other stories I've shared. "I find that this type of collaboration suits me a bit better. Fashion and the arts have so many introverts, and we can't do everything by ourselves. We need to team up and bring the whole vision together, but it's incredibly challenging, especially when we don't have the natural love of talking; but we still have to collaborate to get it there and have it be successful." I think recognizing that a lot of people are introverted is important. I feel that often extroverts can overpower introverts simply because we love to chat and can go on and on. Being able to recognize that not everyone shares this desire or ability is important because otherwise introverts' voices and ideas may get lost or overpowered.

For Amy and her team working on her pajama brand, she shared some of the ways they manage to collaborate without pushing themselves into an intensely social space. "We tend to prepare agendas with our talking points, and since we're all working remotely right now, we have a Google doc and everyone has a section to prepare the talking points they want to go through. This gives us time throughout the week to collect our thoughts, and it helps us to stay on track. Given all of our temperaments, we may have struggled to think of those on the spot." I like how pre-planning is one way to put social stress at ease. The planning aspect is critical, and extroverts could take a page or two from this. As much value comes from on-the-spot conversations, there is definitely something to be said about having pre-planned points to stay on track. Just like anything, it's about striking that balance. Amy said that this ability to pre-plan "elevates the quality of thinking" within her team.

Despite this ability to handle and work on an introverted team, Amy is no stranger to the environment of extroverts. "It's a complete opposite of what we were doing with Print Fresh: there, we had a really outgoing team of people-persons who loved traveling, and now the types of meetings and the energy is totally different. A lot of it is e-commerce, so it's super-prepared internet content." It goes to show how different environments and modes of operation suit different personalities better. This is great to keep in mind when we are looking at defining roles within a collaborative setting, and part of that might even include identifying who the introverts and extroverts are and finding roles that suit those varied temperaments. "We will draft things and photograph them, and once we had a chance to work alone, we begin that collaborative process, and the collaboration isn't even necessarily verbal. It's a lot of collecting and group chatting and nonverbal collaboration." In the chapter before, we learned from Kristy Leone how nonverbal collaboration can help unleash a whole new type of creativity. In the same sense, nonverbal or nontraditional collaboration can give introverted temperaments a bigger place to express their ideas and really have their *voices* heard.

Leo, Amy's partner in both marriage and business, is extremely extroverted, and he helps Amy to collaborate as an introvert. "That partnership of Leo and I together and being so differently inclined has really led us to be so successful. We really need that mixture of two different temperaments working together, and we can both fill in for each other's weaknesses." In the same way that within your team you can recognize each other's temperaments and play to those strengths, it may be just as important to find a partner or team that has both—if you don't have it already. Essentially, introverts are still collaborating in a great way—it just looks different from the typical idea of a team sitting around a table all spitballing ideas. Whether you're introverted or extroverted, it will serve you well to utilize multiple modes of communication of ideas to maximize the creative potential of your team. You want to accommodate all temperaments so no ideas are left unsaid.

VERSATILITY AND ADAPTABILITY WITH THE HOMESTEAD & KYLE SCHACHNER

In any collaborative setting, you need to keep an open mind and allow for things to shift and change as new ideas and opportunities present themselves. Making steadfast decisions can often inhibit the evolution of spaces. Caitlyn Deviney from The Homestead, a creative space in Glenside, Pennsylvania, shared her sentiments about this openness when sharing her story. Caitlyn and her collaborative partner, Ben Morris, are both musicians, but they also found themselves facilitating and cultivating spaces for people to share their artistic endeavors and build authentic connections. It started out with small gatherings for music, poetry, and general storytelling, and now these spaces have evolved into their permanent space, The Homestead, which has become a consistent and permanent platform for all sorts of creatives to share and express their art.

It all started with monthly gatherings and potlucks that facilitated "creative sharing time." This brought in art and creations from all different platforms and so many different people, some of whom just wanted to come and absorb and others who had plans to share their work and ideas. Caitlyn and Ben found that they had opened up a dialogue in an organic way as they were hosting these spaces. Within these gatherings, people were able to share art and talk about it, and it began to spiral into conversations about harder things happening in people's lives and in the world.

"It was empowering and organic," Caitlyn said, and they fostered hard conversations—not arguments. These meetings continued to grow, and eventually, word of mouth about these gatherings led to people driving for hours to come to Caitlyn and Ben's backyard. After a few years, Caitlyn and Ben decided they wanted to find a larger physical space to host and hold events. They began reaching out to their community about where they should find a new space; no one wanted them to go far. Without even realizing it, their idea had shifted into something their community truly valued.

They found their space and were met with wild success, which allowed them to do more than they anticipated. They did a lot of work and had friends do work for them—it was a community effort to make the new space beautiful and inspiring. Caitlyn and Ben helped each other with everything from the initial remodel to building their website and creating their business plan. "I don't think that I would be able to do this without Ben and his different skills and assets; we complement each other and play to our strengths very well. We are able to make this what it is because we have this dynamic duo situation going on," Caitlyn told me. This dichotomy in their partnership makes the space as versatile as it can be because they can offer different services and skills.

Ben has a recording studio in the back, and now he can offer his services in their space. He brings in more diversity to the gathering place by encouraging musicians and spoken-word artists to use the space. Caitlyn, on the other hand, has a natural tendency to host and has a personable and hospitable attitude that sets the vibe in the room. "It was hard to figure out exactly what we wanted, and it got complicated at trying to weigh the options, and there were times when the options were definitely on the side of 'I don't know if that idea matches my vision.'" This is important to keep in mind: while being versatile and willing to adapt is important, that versatility and adaptability still needs to relate to your ultimate vision and mission.

"We were always keeping in the back of our brains that we need to make this as versatile as possible—because if something was permanent, it might limit what could go on in here." Keeping that idea of versatility in mind allowed for conscious decision making to take place. It also allows for things to change as they learn what the needs of their business are, given that they only opened in January 2020. "When creating a venue, any decision needs to be in theory changeable and reversible." Not locking yourself in gives you more room for mistakes to be easily eradicated and limits the 'make-it-or-break-it' mentality that a lot of businesses face. A majority of businesses don't make it past two years, so Caitlyn and Ben have worked hard to ensure success by leaning into that ability to adapt and change.[19] Success can come about in surprising ways, and you hear lots of creatives indicating that their original idea has shifted greatly from their initial plan. Ben and Caitlyn have already worked this potential into their business plan, avoiding the need to do so in the future.

KYLE SCHACHNER

Kyle Schachner works at a software development firm with a team that designs various types of software for business use. Between his team's system of interval adjustments and his own role as the "translator," Kyle engages with collaboration daily. This constant use of collaboration has sharpened Kyle's skills as a salesman, teammate, and professional in ways that can easily be adjusted from the tech sphere to any creative role. As we dive into Kyle's story, consider how his methods could translate into your own work.

Using his studies of communications, advertising, and public relations, Kyle is able to serve as the middleman between multiple parties doing business together. He represents his tech firm when he approaches businesses, but what is unique to him is the ability to understand different personalities and what mode of communication he needs to use in order to reach people at either end of the bargain. Kyle's experience working with creative people in the arts, creative people in tech, and businesspeople in his professional career helped him learn how to communicate with lots of different groups and refine those skills to make himself an asset to his company.

---

19   Katie Horne, "Scary (But True) Small Business Statistics You Can't Afford To Ignore," (Digital.com, August 25, 2020), https://digital.com/small-business-statistics/.

"I had different roles throughout my career so far, and so through that experience, I turned myself into an information broker. I am the middleman between multiple parties, and my unique benefit to my team is that I know and understand different personalities and types of communication that need to happen." That's an interesting part of collaboration that we haven't engaged with yet—this idea of translating across platforms and professions. For Kyle, one side of his business uses executive conversation, and then he translates that into software conversations he has with his team. "People live in the center of their own world, the human condition operates in that way, and our default is to look at the world from our perspective and how it relates to us. When I am collaborating, it is so essential that I take in the opinions and perspectives of other people and really internalize them to learn how other people will interpret how these ideas are expressed." Whether Kyle is talking to a client or his team, it is crucial the information and language he uses is clear to them so the collaboration aspect can really take shape. You can't collaborate if you aren't on the same page.

This refined communication ability quickly gave Kyle an opportunity as he began to fall into the world of technology and software. I struggle a lot with tech terminology, and Kyle shared that a lot of businesspeople do, too. They might know how to use their tech, but what they don't realize is how inefficient some existing systems are. "I research their company and see what problems we need to solve by making tools for them, and then we use those tools to help the company become more efficient." It's basically like having a tech wizard come in and give you an update you didn't know you needed. "You would be shocked at how inefficient some companies are in regard to their technology. The processes some people are using online are so old and dated, and there is no need for it. There are way better and more efficient ways to operate." So as Kyle and his team analyze their clients and begin to build new technology for them, collaboration kicks in again.

Building software, Kyle shares, "is a really fluid process." Within his team, they operate by doing small tasks in short bursts and then pausing to reassess. "Instead of taking big bites, we take small bites. We reassess and reiterate so that we have greater agility and changes can happen faster and more efficiently." That environment and philosophy lends itself to teamwork and collaboration explicitly because it allows for a myriad of opportunities to change, adopt new ideas, and have conversations. When you work with so many different types of people, there are opportunities for teaching and learning (collaboration) and opportunities to adopt new ideas.

Say you work on a project for six months with your team. It's refined and finalized, and then you bring it to your client only to find out that it's not what they had in mind. This leaves you in a bind where time, resources, and potentially money have been wasted. Now consider breaking that six-month project into two-week intervals, and touch base with your client every two to four weeks.

Now you can get feedback.

This opens up the floor to adjust what you are doing if something doesn't work, bring more people into the conversation, and ultimately not waste or ruin resources. It's a more sustainable means of creation. "It creates more space for collaboration and adjustment because we have more opportunities for conversations about what we are doing and what effective changes might look like."

Short-term goals and mini deadlines allow a project to become more inclusive, more flexible, and ultimately more successful and collaborative. That is especially true in the current climate right now. Given the rise of COVID-19, Kyle's team was able to adjust accordingly because their planning spanned for shorter intervals: they didn't have an entire six-month operation disrupted, but rather a two-week deadline that could then be adjusted to meet the new normal. "The world is constantly changing, and any industry that you are in needs to be able to constantly change. What works right now may not work in a couple months, so having that agility to adjust to the short term allows you to account for an ever-changing world and industry." That is extremely simple yet profound if you take a moment to consider it. This mode of collaboration really allows for you to get blindsided and still come out on top.

I can't stress enough that we have to focus on the present. It is essential to plan, project, analyze, and take the future into account, and that can inform what we will do right now, but at the end of the day, no one knew the coronavirus was going to completely change the way of life for humans across the globe. Businesses are packed for resources, so when you focus on the short term, you can use the best resources of everyone who is part of the team.

FIGURING IT OUT AND MAKING IT HAPPEN WITH COLSAC SKIERS

———

Inspiration can come from anywhere, and when it strikes, it's important to recognize it and act on it. That's exactly what Travis Lukens did when he founded Colsac Skiers. "I love to water ski, and one morning, I watched a news program and saw some man coming back from Afghanistan. His arms were blown off in an explosion, and his passion was kayaking. The news story shared how he was fitted with prosthetic arms, and eventually he got to go kayaking again. It made me wonder if we could somehow get him waterskiing." You see, everything is new...until it's not. Travis and I spoke about the duty we have as humans to create new things and just figure "it" out. Travis got in touch with a lady in Florida who had some experience taking people with disabilities waterskiing. "She invited me to Florida to ski with a thirteen-year-old boy with spina bifida, and as I waterskied alongside of him, he had the biggest smile on his face, and I was hooked." Travis has served as a pilot for most of his professional life, and he didn't have any experience starting a company, let alone an adaptive waterskiing school. It is important to recognize what you don't know and use the resources you have to figure it out.

From this seed of an idea and a passion for serving this specific community, Travis started his adaptive waterskiing school, based in Wisconsin. "I wanted to start this company, but I didn't know what I needed to do." Travis started reaching out to some of his connections—a buddy from high school who is now a lawyer, his cousin's husband who is a professional water skier—and slowly he began to build a network of experienced people to help him get started.

"For me, it was all about sharing my level of waterskiing with people who can't go themselves." This passion project turned into a nonprofit business because of collaboration. "I always had someone guiding me through things when I had no idea what I was doing." Travis relied on his connections to help him make more connections, and eventually he had a board of directors and started to really get the ball rolling. His inspiration was enough for him to start collaborating with others to figure out what he didn't know and eventually get Colsac Skiers off the ground.

Despite not knowing initially how to start a company, Travis made it work. He and his coworkers never know what challenges each person brings, but they figure out the best way to accommodate them. "This is adaptive sports, so we just adapt, and we will figure it out." This can be applied to any collaborative venture, not just sports. Anytime you work together with people, you have to identify what the challenges are and learn how to work around them. There might be one end goal, but there can be so many different ways to achieve it. It is extremely important to identify which path to the end goal will work best for you, your team, and your unique challenges.

With no formal training working with people with disabilities, Travis was really throwing himself into uncharted territory. His only formal expertise was how to do it safely—but the safety regulations don't teach you about the minds of the people. "The first time we worked with a kid with autism, it was really challenging. Then we realized this type of work isn't about 'easy;' we are in this for the challenge. We read a lot about autism. We brought them on, then we made it work. Just a bit of adjusted mechanics and all of a sudden these kids are capable of doing incredible things." The approach Travis and his team took here is remarkable. Rather than limiting their services, they decided to rise to the challenge, find out what they didn't know, and create an experience for a person who otherwise would not have been able to have it. The access to information we have is astounding; we just have to use it.

Travis shared a story about a fourteen-year-old boy who fell from a tree and broke his back. The boy loved surfing, but he was unable to surf after his injury. They collected materials and built a surfboard to accommodate this boy. "That was one where we didn't necessarily know what the best way to do it was, but we just gave it a try and it worked great." Travis and his team figured out how to get him surfing again. Colsac Skiers uses sports equipment from a manufacturer in Florida that makes sit skis. Some of their equipment comes from their own designs, and some of it is adapted from what's available.

This idea of being adaptive and looking for solutions when they aren't obvious translates so clearly into all creative endeavors. Colsac Skiers saw a gap in water sports, so they got creative, reached out to their network, and filled in that gap. No matter what limits you, whether it is physical restrictions, supplies, money, or access, you can find a way forward. They weren't always buying brand-new equipment for their students because sometimes the equipment didn't exist. They took what they had, looked at their challenges, and created what they needed. This was not only creative but extremely collaborative. There are a myriad of opportunities and ideas about how to achieve goals, and they need to be utilized. Your team has lots of different ideas and ways to tackle your different challenges, and by collaborating you can rise to them, overcome them, and potentially create something new. It is all about having an "I can do this" attitude and not taking failure as a sign to give up.

CULTURAL AWARENESS WITH JON KUYPER

Film Producer Jon Kuyper, most known for his work on *Mad Max: Fury Road* (2015), *The Great Gatsby* (2013) and *The Hunger Games: Mockingjay - Part 1* (2014), is in a field that couldn't exist without collaboration. There are so many moving parts in the film industry and so many visions that need to come together. In these large-scale collaborative settings, Kuyper shared the importance of going the extra mile. It's important to set yourself apart when you can so easily get lost in the crowd. Someone needs to bring it all together and coordinate the collaboration when it gets this big. That's Jon's role.

The film industry is full of travel and collaboration. As a young English literature major, Jon had a few options as he was graduating: law school, teaching, or politics, he thought. None of these ideas really resonated with Jon and what he wanted for himself—the top of the list being located on the West Coast. "I realized that geographically, none of those would work for me because lifestyle-wise I wanted to be in SoCal." So for a young writer in Southern California, there was one obvious option: entertainment. "My father had some contacts there, so I had an easy in. I was anticipating writing or working with writers because of my literature major and concentration in creative writing, and so I started working for a talent agency: I was reading scripts and rating them. I would use this to help the agents limit how many scripts they needed to read. Based on my ratings, they read the interesting scripts and just got covers of the others. That is where I started, and to supplement my income I was working as a production assistant."

That role as a production assistant was a crucial part of Jon's career development, because that is where he fell in love with producing. "It's a very collaborative process, and I was working with every department; I kept moving up and eventually moved into the role of an assistant director as well as work on some odd jobs in various departments. Its art, but business, and in a way, manufacturing and construction. The different departments are all collaborating and pulling together to reach the end goal." From the beginning, Jon was working in lots of departments and becoming more versatile and collaborating between departments. All of this led Jon to his current role in some impressive films.

Working on films, you may have a team of one hundred to one hundred and twenty-five people who all have different skills. Everyone is working together, fulfilling their roles in harmony, and more or less waiting for their moment to make their mark on the process. Jon moved away from writing and went forward with production. "Something unique about my position is that it's not necessarily creative. I work as a line producer, so I focus on keeping track of the budget and building and managing the schedule and coordinating all of the different moving parts and people. I am the person that bridges all of them and makes them all come together."

Jon is the collaboration coordinator, if you will. "I don't view it as a creative position, but it is in the creative world; I have a more administrative role in it. It is uniquely suited to me because I am really creative, and to really fulfill my role I need to understand the creative people in the project, which requires a certain amount of creative capacity, but the business aspect is really natural to me, too. I feel like I fell into producing for this reason." Being able to balance the creativity and the business aspect is challenging, but Jon is able to translate between the two worlds and the two different types of vocabulary and advocate for each of them and their creative desires in a corporate setting.

The creative vision can sometimes get compromised when business comes into play. This is where collaboration is important: you need to bring both points of view to the table. "I always look at filmmaking like building a building because there are similarities in the multitude of departments all coming together to create the finished product." Jon allows the creative people to do their work, and he manages the moving parts to make sure the bank and the timeline are on track so the creatives can focus on what they do best. This directly correlates to the importance of defining roles that we discussed with Adam Simone and his company, Leaf Shave, in Part Two.

Jon's work has taken him all over the world, and something he has observed is how different cultures approach these collaborative settings. "The American filmmaking culture and work ethic is very unique and quite strong, and there are almost always Americans somewhere in the mix; I think a lot of that is because a lot of Americans are spearheading these film projects." In this sense, Jon has seen that people who really embrace this work ethic set themselves apart. He would certainly be the one to notice, too, because he has the role of coordinating this collaboration. "The people that have become successful are the people who go the extra mile." The film industry really took off in the US, so initially there weren't many incentives abroad for work with film. As this slowly shifted and the industry began to spread out, people within the countries that the industry was spreading to began adopting some of the methods of the film industry and negotiate them with their own cultural customs.

"In the states in Florida, they have many more lightning strikes annually than the rest of the US combined; when a thunderstorm comes through, everyone knows what to do and how to respond, whereas in South Africa its very windy, so the crew knows how to accommodate their tents and lighting to prep for the given scenarios." While the *local* crew knows how to prep for these, Jon shared an experience that highlights how the crews that travel to these locations don't know how to accommodate as quickly. "In Louisiana it's so hot and humid and there are so many mosquitos, so in the afternoon they come out. I would see crew members bring up little mesh nets and didn't know what they were for until I was immediately attacked by the bugs." That goes to show how different places assimilate to their environments, and there is a big opportunity for learning from different cultures.

"You can learn incredible things from the different cultures."

JON KUYPER

In Los Angeles, Jon shared how the industry moves so quickly and at such a fast pace, which other countries are not as accustomed to because their cultural priorities are different from that of LA. "When I was in Serbia, for instance, we needed to build a stone fireplace for a set. Our Serbian crew members were hand-making it in rock and cementing it together, whereas in the states we would make a fake one and special-effects the fire in. You can learn incredible things from the different cultures, although I found that it was challenging to come from the American work ethic and then go to other countries who have different modes of production." This challenge Jon is articulating can happen in a myriad of situations, not just within the film industry. It's important to consider when collaborating how your collaborators work and consider where to give and take. "Often, Americans take leadership roles and motivate people to do things the way we do in LA or the US; you need to understand how they work and adapt to the strengths and weaknesses of the team, and then adapt and work around it." This adaptation is crucial to successfully collaborating, whether it's between cultures or just between two people.

COLLABORATION OVER COMPETITION WITH FORMAL FITNESS TRAINING

———

We live in a society where it feels like everything is a competition. Marketing strategies often suggest that one brand is better than all of the others, and in some ways that has shaped our way of thinking in terms of success. Obtaining success has this idea attached to it that is rooted in the fundamental belief that to be successful you have to be better than everyone else.[20] Why is this something that we hold so closely? I want to challenge this idea and potentially dismantle it with thoughts and ideas from the entrepreneur and author Michael Hartman, whom I had a lovely conversation with about this idea specifically.

---

20   "The Secret To Success: Don't Compete ... Dominate," Business Trends and Insights. https://www.americanexpress.com/en-us/business/trends-and-insights/articles/the-secret-to-success-dont-compete-dominate/.

Mike works as a fitness trainer and, in some ways, a life coach. His mission is focused on becoming one percent better every day, and with fitness and nutrition at the core of this, he also advocates for things like money management, healthy relationships, and strong mental health. His business model is focused on the idea of perpetual improvement, including the pursuit of health, wealth, success, happiness, and great personal relationships. In 2011, Mike was a trainer at L.A. Fitness, and one of his clients encouraged him to start his own business. In the fitness world, there are so many different types of trainers, gyms, and boutiques, which creates a lot of competition. It was important to Mike that he narrow down his mission and craft his business. That was his first taste of professional collaboration. His paralegal client could see how the corporate business world was draining him, and she helped him take the first steps in changing his career path.

Mike shared with me how his clients became like family, and as he developed working relationships with all different types of clients, he started to see that people really believed in him and his mission. Whether or not Mike knew it back then, he was already embodying that perpetual improvement mindset for both himself and his clients. Mike shared that his clients "showed me that people who are successful are not all snobby and uptight. They really care about me and other people and helped me see that you can actually be both." Your momentum has to come from somewhere, and for Mike, that momentum came from his clients. The support and faith they had in him is ultimately what inspired him to help people grow and do better and really achieve the lifestyles they want and deserve.

I was able to interview one of his earliest clients who was with him during his switch from L.A. Fitness to his own business, and she said, "He had so much to offer his clients; his focus was improving himself and becoming better at his job, and it was easy to recognize that desire. He made his clients have that same mindset, and really pushed me. He had more confidence in me than I had in myself, and it made all the difference." By encouraging people to believe in their ability to reach their fitness goals, he helped them boost their self-confidence and join the perpetual improvement movement.

Now, where does Formal Fitness Training fit into the ideas driving creative collaboration and arts entrepreneurship? In our interview, Mike said, "I look at fitness as an art form because I am crafting workout and nutrition programs." Even more than that, I would argue Mike is curating people's lives. He is looking at his clients, helping them pinpoint where they are falling short, and encouraging them and collaborating with them to identify the steps they need to take to be successful. "Younger guys are looking up to me and wondering how I did certain things to alleviate my debt, have a successful relationship with my wife, and achieve things like buying a new car. These people made me realize that I was achieving things that a lot of people didn't think were possible. Now I'm trying to make those things possible for lots of people."

"Early on in starting a business, the key is to say yes and always show up for other people and businesses and help them be successful. Donate time and support for your friends who are opening businesses and offering opportunities to people who are interested but don't have anything to judge you off of." Mike says this is one of the major things that helped his business succeed once he got the ball rolling. There is plenty of room and plenty of money out there for everyone to be successful, and for this reason, Mike believes "competition hurts and collaboration helps." Approaching any sort of project, whether it's opening a business, painting a mural, or writing a book, it's important to keep in mind that other people have tackled things similar to what you might be looking to do. Knowing this and understanding your industry, then, gives way to potentially meeting and working with people who know how to do what it is you want to do. Rather than being in competition, you can work together to make everyone's visions come to fruition.

Collaboration can lead to success when it replaces the deeply rooted notion that being the best or competing within the industry is the only way to be at the top. Do what you are good at and put your mark on it and your customers. Mike and I touched on this idea of approaching the same things in different ways when we discussed the different types of diets and workouts that emerge in the nutrition and fitness fields. "I do understand why people like certain things even if I don't agree with them. See if it works for you, give it twenty-one days, and decide if it really works for you and your lifestyle. As long as people are approaching me with an open mind and making sure everyone is welcome, I am not opposed to hearing what they have to say."

In a field as broad as exercise, very few people will be doing it all the same, and this is what Mike stressed. Just because someone is doing it differently doesn't mean it's a bad thing. That is why it is better to collaborate than to compete—you can allow people to choose what works for them and support them in doing it. This translates into any industry, especially the arts. Methodologies are constantly changing, emerging, and evolving, and we don't necessarily have to fear this; we just need to embrace what works for us and do it right.

Mike thinks of lifestyle as a sort of scale from zero to one hundred. This scale represents the dichotomies of doing different things in different ways, zero and one hundred being the extremes. "You wanna live in that middle 60 percent. You can gravitate to one side or the other but being able to stay balanced in the middle is what works for me." This is important to keep in mind when you work with other people, because everyone falls uniquely on the scale of how they choose to do things. You need to approach each person with respect even if you don't align perfectly.

Mike exemplifies that there is plenty of room for everyone to succeed. Approaching something that has been done before isn't necessarily problematic; the question is, how will you make it unique? This is how you avoid professional competition and open the door up to collaborations. "I believe that collaboration over competition is the way to go when building communities, businesses, and your life. I think the partnerships and mutually beneficial collaborations create a multitude of pillars. As one person, we can create only one pillar with what we are personally capable of; together we can create many pillars, then put them together and create an amazing foundation for a castle." By collaborating among similar fields, you actually begin to strengthen the entire industry.

Mike says, "Especially in fitness, I found that my business would not be what it is if I was not constantly trying to elevate the company I surround myself with, along with key partnerships I have." By working with other businesses and helping them succeed, you open up the opportunity to learn, make connections, and create a cycle of showing up for each other all within the same industry. This idea isn't much different from painters visiting each other's exhibitions and buying each other's work or the collaborative efforts in films or music.

My major takeaway with my time with Mike is this idea of embracing collaboration with people who you might initially see as competition and also being confident in what you uniquely have to bring to the table. Balance and hard work are pillars in the fitness community, but they also translate into the world of arts entrepreneurship. It is up to you to define what your path looks like and really go after it by finding balance and working hard. There is a lot left to chance in these situations, but hard work and balance can allow you to take control of a lot. As we wrapped up, Mike shared, "You can't choose everything in your life, but you get to choose friends and partnerships." And to that I would include, you can choose your collaborators as well.

STAYING CURRENT THROUGH COLLABORATION WITH DAVID GUINN

———

"As someone who has been an artist for a long time, it's really impressive to see just how crucial collaboration was in shaking my career up."

DAVID GUINN

David Guinn, a renowned muralist from Philadelphia, always knew art was his calling, but he wasn't sure how that career would be possible for him. When he was just getting started, the mural arts program was just beginning, too. David saw that opportunity, and what happened next with his career followed organically. Collaboration can literally transform careers, as David will attest to. His involvement with mural arts felt temporary as he contemplated the idea of attending grad school or pursuing work in architecture, and according to David, "That's been the case for twenty years now."

When David was beginning, they didn't really have programs to study the educational side of the arts, which David now plays a role in. He gained most of his experience through apprenticeships and having mentors. For David, it was a very informal process that came about through friendships, introductions, and working for different people over the years. "I really learned a ton, and I still think about all of the things I learned when I was only twenty-four, really young." The word "artist" for David came with a type of identity and pretension that he was wary of, so for a long time he would identify as a painter, but now, David realizes that while he is in fact a painter, he is an artist through and through.

Artists always have this battle of maintaining their own unique style but also trying to stay current. It is natural for artists to look at what others are doing and what is in popular demand. The way David stays current is through collaboration. In 2016, he worked on the Electric Street project in Philadelphia. "We had this little wall, and it was really wide open, and people said, 'I think you should incorporate lighting.' And so they introduced me to a lighting artist, and neither of us really knew what we were gonna do. He suggested that we use a specific material because it resembles neon and it matches my colorful style. We just sort of came up with this plan and then it totally transformed my career."

After that wildly successful project, David got linked up with Arcadia University, and that is how I came to work with him in 2017 and 2018. We began the Arcadia Public Art Project, and David was our professor. After we finished both of the murals, we ended up incorporating lights in the same way David had at Electric Street. "Most of the work that I've done since Electric Street has involved this lighting, and most of the interest in my work more recently has been because it involves a new dimension. I had never worked with electricity, but I wouldn't have gotten involved with it or ever thought to have used it unless it was in that collaborative setting."

David shared that most of his projects over the past four years have happened because of ideas that developed through collaboration. Having an idea develop that no one would have developed on their own is so exciting. "I had been painting murals for fifteen years, and I felt like I had reached this plateau. I didn't know how to keep growing by doing what I was doing. And then this collaboration allowed that growth to happen." David's story is so remarkable because it shows how truly powerful and transformational collaboration is. The creativity develops in a whole new way, and the opportunity to learn new skills and processes that you may never have found alone is so important. This could move the whole art world forward in a new direction if collaboration is more widely utilized and embraced the way it is with David.

As all of this collaboration began to come into David's career, so did his role teaching at Arcadia University. David began working with students, and he said how working with young students has kept his ideas fresh. The process of creating murals with the students gave him the chance to learn so many new tools to collaborate that he had never used before while working alone. That collaborative process with students was extremely satisfying for David, too. "The satisfaction from working on the murals all together was really cool. And it felt great. At the end of each semester, I felt really connected with all the students. I felt like we were on a trip together; it was similar to how you feel after going to summer camp or something—we were bonded. That doesn't always happen on projects, but to have this camaraderie and that unique bond is really cool." Collaboration creates amazing projects, but it also creates a great feeling. The accomplishments that emerge from collaboration are so remarkable. There is the combination, for David, of a creative success as well as an emotional advantage.

By collaborating, David was able to step into roles that he didn't always think were for him. "I never saw myself as a natural leader," David shared. "In fact, I gravitated toward these isolated environments because I didn't have to fulfill those roles." After he began working with Arcadia students, however, that shifted. I can speak from experience and say that David is one of the best leaders I have ever worked for. There is a unique balance leaders must find between taking charge and delegation, and David did so perfectly. He allowed each one of his apprentices (myself included) to find what role worked for us and to run with it. "It was really cool to be a leader, though, because through my leadership others were empowered to be leaders. I just loved how different people found their strengths and contributed in different ways. I was glad to help develop a project where I could think about the student experience specifically."

I am a natural leader, and David encouraged this nature of mine and brought me back on the project the second year in a leadership role. Intuition served him well with his students, because he could sense where people were comfortable and allowed them to thrive there, but he also pushed them just enough to try new things and support the different roles. This collaborative project brought so many different dimensions to David's career. "As someone who has been an artist for a long time, it's really impressive to see just how crucial collaboration was in shaking my career up." People settle into their routine and begin to fall into patterns. The way to break those patterns is by collaborating. David is a perfect example of how it can refresh your entire career.

COLLATERAL COLLABORATION WITH MATT D'ARRIGO

———

Matt D'Arrigo, the founder of ARTS in San Diego, California, was starting to feel burned out in his role as CEO. When he created ARTS, his passion was fueled off of that for a long time. But at a certain level, that passion began to plateau, and Matt wanted to use his strength of creation and shift gears. Matt made the choice to leave ARTS and wound up in a role at the Clare Rose Foundation—one of ARTS' major funders—and his job now is focused on having conversations with leaders across the country about how to maintain programs like ARTS.

"While I was still at ARTS, I was being invited into conversations at the national level about national creative youth development. Lots of organizations were all doing this work, but they were systemically underfunded or under supplied. They started a conversation with leaders around the country and started discussing how to maintain these programs. At each meeting there were new people, challenging conversations, and the difficulty of convening large groups of people. These conversations were getting me excited and energizing me. I knew I wanted to go into this direction of addressing this issue." Matt is now the director of creative youth development for the Clare Rose Foundation in San Diego, and his role is to engage with lots of different organizations and figure out how to help them maintain their programs. These conversations have a big impact and lead to the ripple effect. One drop can spread and turn into a wave. I call this collateral collaboration: by simply encouraging people to work together and giving them the tools to do it, they will continue the collaboration in many different ways. This is really important because it shows how powerful just one collaborative act may be. It has a domino effect.

By working with the Clare Rose Foundation, Matt is able to create programming for these arts leaders and give them workshops and training opportunities for professional development. This then allows the youth they work with to have better allies with proper education and training. The network Matt has created will figure out what they want to learn, and Matt helps foster this assistance to achieve this education. At these meetings, all of these leaders came up with pillars for youth development programs. Those pillars primarily rely on professional development, storytelling in order to expand, and building and expanding pathways to funding and resources. In order to make all the different arts organizations around the country successful, these pillars needed to be addressed and made successful. This is no easy undertaking, however;

as Matt remarked, "This involves creating systematic changes and government policies to open up resources."

However, this big conversation opened up the door for collaboration and collective opportunity. "The key to implementing this blueprint was to create cross-sector networks: looking at local and regional leaders to create these networks of organizations and community partners, and anyone who has an expertise and resources, and get them all around the table." Matt focuses on establishing these networks and bringing together all types of creatives, community partners, and funders in order to support the mission: creative youth development. When it comes to pathways to funding, the Clare Rose Foundation has already created a network of trained people, and they connect these organizations to funders who are all working together. All of a sudden this massive collaboration has begun, and it doesn't stop with Matt. By convening groups of like-minded individuals and assisting that first step into collaboration, Matt has seen these organizations collaborate on their own.

Patience is something Matt and I discussed in depth, because when you're working with organizations that are struggling sometimes to stay afloat, "there is a sense of urgency, but also the need to have patience." That patience is key in any collaboration, but especially when you are looking to see the effects of the ripple. Matt also shared that in these collaborative practices, "the key to collaboration is trust; nothing can happen collectively or collaboratively without trust." This makes sense, because within collaboration there are varying degrees of power dynamics, which is why we already identified the importance of defining roles. Defining roles helps to eliminate some of these power dynamics and also helps to build that trust, which forms as people adhere to their roles. Defining roles is easy when everyone ultimately has the same vision. This is why collateral collaboration is something Matt has seen a lot of.

In order to really support the youth and their creative development, all of these organizations need to be strong and robust, so recognizing that same ultimate vision while acknowledging different ideas of how to get there is key. "We need to look beyond ourselves individually and look at the collective: going at it alone is so hard, we see that collaborating is a necessity, and we are willing to look beyond individual work to realize that ultimate vision." Rather than looking for some sort of credit or recognition for starting this momentum, Matt is happy to support and then see the effects without being named directly for them. He looks past his own role and sees the collective vision that all of these arts programs are looking to create for their community.

THE SUM OF YOUR EXPERIENCE WITH VAUGHAN LEWIS CARMEN

———

"I've been living a collaborative lifestyle since college," says Vaughan Lewis Carmen, a men's footwear designer who has worked with some of the biggest names in footwear, including Reebok, Converse, and Adidas. The real beginning was in high school: while most of his friends focused on soccer, Carmen focused equally on sports *and* art. He kept trying to merge his passions, and that's what brought him to study at Rhode Island School of Design, where he studied fashion and apparel but also played basketball. College in many ways pulls you in different directions—you learn about new career options, meet mentors, and branch out into new opportunities. The major formative opportunity Carmen seized was the opportunity to study footwear and car design in Italy during his junior year. This inspired him to pursue graduate school in the Netherlands to study the full range of footwear design.

"That's where things got interesting for me, because collaborative projects were always something I wanted to do: I loved people and sports culture, and that was the environment I really saw myself in." Carmen met an alumni designer, Gavin Angel, from his school who he really admired, and they had a conversation where it really clicked: " I can do this and study this, and I don't have to be a traditional designer; I just need to find a middle ground and play to my strengths and know what I bring to the table."

While Carmen was trying to decide what to do for his senior thesis, he was inspired by the alumni basketball tournament where an opportunity came to him. Gavin Angel, an alum, offered Carmen an opportunity at Converse for six months.

"They brought in designers and gave them access to their facilities and let them make whatever they wanted." Carmen jumped on the opportunity in 2017, and that was his first taste of the professional design world. "I was a contracted designer doing whatever I wanted and whatever interested me." This opportunity gave Carmen the chance to learn what his strengths were as well as test out new ideas without any repercussions. He had access to incredible design space and supplies, and all he had to do was focus on creation. "Collaboration was really active in my role there, and it didn't seem like work. We had all this equipment and material at our disposal, so without having to worry about access to the materials needed to create, collaboration happened naturally."

Carmen worked with top designers in this field, and as he created his own designs, he was taking cues from the best. He brought his strengths to the table but also allowed his mentors to show him the ropes. He was getting positive feedback, so he went ahead and created a mock collection with Converse, and what developed from that project was an in-depth experience with the process of show design. As he wrapped up his time with Converse, Carmen then went on to work with Adidas. He worked in their maker lab, and after his stay there he moved on to Reebok. Carmen will finish out his year at Reebok in the summer of 2020 and then is moving to the Netherlands to start working as a leather designer. "I will be in a collaborative environment and working on education and design," says Carmen about his new position in the Netherlands. The design world is inherently collaborative, but the ability to show up with a good sense of your strengths *and* weaknesses can help collaborations flow seamlessly.

For young collaborators who struggle with identifying their strengths, fitting into in a professional environment can feel intimidating. Carmen explained: "I think it's challenging when you are in an unfamiliar space aware that you are the one that is the least experienced in the field. I had to accept that I didn't have all of the answers and that these guys knew more than me and had more experience." I have certainly experienced this feeling throughout the process of writing this book, as well as in my teaching career. Everyone is a novice at some point...even the experts. "I had to go in and take notes on everything and ask so many questions, meet everyone I could, and take every opportunity there was to learn something." It's okay to be the new guy, it's okay to be the novice, it's okay to be the apprentice. It's such an important part of your journey. The mistake Carmen avoided was going in thinking he knew all the answers. Instead, he saw the value in learning from the pros and didn't overestimate his own skill set. There is a fine line between confidence and cockiness. Confidence allows you to enter the room as a novice, own that role, ask the right questions, and bring your creativity and skills to the table. That's exactly what Carmen did, and it brought him around to three of the leading footwear companies in sports. That discomfort and learning curve led to a lot of future successes.

Carmen has now gotten a significant amount of experience under his belt and gotten a taste for what his skills, interests, and goals are. Reebok has served him well, but his choice to move to the Netherlands speaks directly to this idea of knowing what you bring to the table. Carmen realized that when you are working for a big brand like Reebok there is an ultimate "vision" that needs to be met—it's about the branding of these massive companies. He has gotten to the point where he wants his designs to stand on their own and stand out. This also ties into the chapter about large and small-scale collaborations and the idea of credit. Ultimately, his choice to move to the Netherlands will give him more freedom with his ability to create and design. "I think my experiences this far will help me with collaborating because people are drawn to your expertise." What you have done, who you have worked with, where you have been, that all adds to what you bring to the table and what you can offer in your collaborations. The more experiences you have had, the more you speak to.

"I have a story, and all the parts of my story are with the big brands, and those connections certainly help. Now, with the move to Europe, I get to work with a smaller company, but I have more to offer because of my experience." This will be Carmen's first full-time role, and he is planning to stay in the Netherlands for the long term. "I am in a role where I can potentially open collaborations with these artists. You always have those big brands that do collaborations, but there are small places that need to get exposure, and you have to trust small designers who are putting the work." While he loved his time with the "big brands," he wants to shift the narrative from people asking where he worked to asking *what work he did*. He is hoping to empower young designers and engage in spotting talent while working in a smaller-scale operation. "They want my brain committed to their mission." Everyone's brains have different abilities and different things to offer, so when you are collaborating, put a lot of thought into what your brain can bring to the mission and what brains you want committed to your mission.

PLAYING IT COOL
WITH PETER REISS

———

I met Peter Reiss a little over a year ago in Italy. He was visiting one of my roommates, Ellie, and they invited me to tag along on their adventures. One evening over dinner we were getting into a pretty serious conversation about the different tools we have at our fingertips to be "better humans." Among those tools discussed were meditation, healthy eating, therapy, books, technology, friendships—the list is endless. Peter works as a salesman in the rice industry, which has led to extensive travel, lots of business meetings, and a need for collaboration to find success. Our conversation about how he manages his collaborations in the business world really inspired me.

"Collaboration is a fascinating subject. It makes me think of how success is a concept that doesn't come strictly from the force of the individual, but it has a lot to do with luck and with the people you choose to surround yourself with in the environment you want to be successful in." These relationships that you choose to form with people as you join an environment are collaborations. Relationships are naturally collaborative. There is a degree of give and take in any relationship, and collaboration relies on give and take. "Early on as I was evolving in my career, I got a sense of the importance of collaborating with others and identifying who you want to collaborate with."

Peter attributes a great deal of his success to surrounding himself with the right people and adopting a lot of what they had to offer into his own practice. These people, Peter shared, weren't necessarily colleagues, but actually had a lot to do with the experiences he shared outside of business and then applying those to his work. "I have been working from a home office since 2002, and so how I find collaboration most often is through my interaction with people in my life, and I will talk to them about work." Looking to different people in your network for inspiration, ideas, and collaborative opportunities is so simple, and yet so rarely executed. "I could never have come up with every successful idea without some degree of collaboration." Collaboration is not just about people being together: it's something we have to work at and make happen. It is a practice. "You have to practice it; I have been collaborating for almost my entire career, and I have learned that it can happen naturally in person, but there are different ways to achieve this when you can't be in person, too."

I think this tangent of collaboration is a need even for an autonomous person. As I'm writing this book during the COVID-19 pandemic, our society has gone through a major shift from being together to being apart. Collaboration is not just people being together: it is something you have to foster and reach for. You have to practice it. I have been collaborating from a distance for almost my entire career. It can happen naturally in person, but there are different ways

Peter shared that the main reason he feels collaboration has become a regular practice for him has to do with the fact that he grew up in the 60s. "I remember becoming enamored with a lot of the concepts that emerged from that era that are still resonating today." These ideas, which were seen as radical at the time, are just starting to take shape in society, according to Peter. "One of those ideas was the importance of the environment; another was natural and healthful food; another was the energy attached to music. These ideas that have been in my head for quite some time have really helped me have this open-minded approach in my life and work."

I loved how Peter was able to connect this mindset from the 60s that has taken shape in society some fifty years later and how it has guided him to the place he is at today. That time period was so radical, and it was this quest for new ideas and a new understanding of life. For Peter, a big part of that philosophy was doing things differently, opening up, and allowing things to unfold naturally. This may be part of the reason "hippies" get a bad rap for being so relaxed and chill about everything. "I have adapted that life philosophy and put it into my approach to business. I don't go in with the idea that I need to do anything right away; I try to have a consultative and collaborative approach and try to make it an enjoyable experience." Peter works to create ideas that can be expanded upon. "I don't need to sell you right now; I just need to start the conversation and evolve from there." Have you ever heard of a "chill" businessman? Now you have.

This approach has met Peter with great success in life and business. "This approach to business and collaboration is slightly less traditional, but it really embodies that 60s ethos." There is something really progressive and open minded about approaching business this way. As with any company, it really comes down to the culture, and without the right culture it becomes really difficult to collaborate and see success. "Culture is key to engage in collaboration freely. You need to have awareness of those human qualities that clients or colleagues have and focus on the conversation." By embodying this ethos from the 60s, Peter has found that it puts people at ease, and in turn he has a better ability to work with different personality styles. "People are so different. You have introverts and extroverts, and forward and passive people, and everyone has a style that requires certain circumstances for them to shine. There are certain styles that can send people into back-up mode that may result in a failed business deal."

"It's about being patient, doing some more work on your end, and ultimately being able to see others and meet them where they are at."

PETER REISS

This embodiment of being relaxed allows Peter to get a sense of his clients before choosing how to approach them. "It's about being patient, doing some more work on your end, and ultimately being able to see others and meet them where they are at." The 60s were about challenging the norm, doing things differently, opening up, trying new things, new music, new ways of dressing and engaging in politics, and so much more. "I grew up with hippies and artists on one side and businesspeople on the other. There is a way to be both, and I am driven by that." If you ever have the pleasure of meeting Peter, you will instantly understand this relaxed nature that he so well embodies.

There are so many different approaches you can take to your collaborations. There are endless possibilities, and we have only dipped our toes into the topic with a few wonderful examples. No matter what you bring to the table and no matter what your outcome may be, I encourage you to remember Peter and his 60s ethos. Oftentimes situations seem like they must be win/lose, but this mentality may allow you to think outside the box and generate win/win outcomes. Be patient, be relaxed, and meet people where they are at.

CONCLUSION

THE POWER OF MENTORSHIP WITH JILL PEDERSON

Jill Pederson, associate professor of art history at Arcadia University, is currently in the process of completing her own book manuscript about Leonardo da Vinci, and is a great mentor of mine. I worked closely with Jill throughout my time at Arcadia University, and I took nearly every course she taught. My love and appreciation for Leonardo certainly blossomed in her classroom. She has her BA, her MA, and her PhD in art history and is one of the finest art historians I have had the pleasure of learning and receiving advising from. Having Jill as a mentor and collaborating with her on a lot of my undergraduate work was an extremely important part of shaping my interest and inspirations for this book.

Having grown up in New Mexico, Jill was constantly seeing artwork and was engaging with the history of the artwork in the Southwest. It became an interest that really came to fruition in college. "I started taking art history classes, and then when I studied abroad in Florence, I totally fell in love with art history and changed my major." She admired her professor in undergrad, Claire Bargellini, and took lots of classes with her. When Jill graduated, she decided to move to Milan, improve her Italian, and work in the American Consulate as an intern.

Now fluent in Italian, Jill decided to pursue her masters in art history. She was an intern to David Allan Brown for a summer, and he was one of the first mentors who opened up some doors for Jill as an emerging professional in the world of art history. David, the curator of Italian paintings at the National Gallery of Art in DC, helped Jill get an internship at the National Gallery. Brown had written many books about art history and was well known within the field, so working under him as an intern was a great experience for Jill as someone just emerging into the art history world. She decided after about year or so of working with David to get her PhD in art history.

Jill utilized her network and was connected to Johns Hopkins University. "At Johns Hopkins University I worked with Charles Dempsey and Stephen Campbell—when I got there it was very rigorous." Jill described her advisors as old school and tough, but in a great way that "held me to a very high standard." Those high standards are no doubt a factor in the success she has had since working with them. "Collaborating with my advisors was an honor. Dempsey had such a long history within the field. His advisor was Panofsky, a revered German art historian. "Then Campbell was the new, young superstar, and I had this amazing combination of the older tradition and the new emerging methodologies, which brought really important aspects to the conversations surrounding the arts." Her advisors embodied these contrasting yet complimentary ideologies, which allowed Jill to adopt her own methods as she was becoming a historian. Having those two advisors during her time there really allowed Jill to become the historian she is today: meticulous, organized, and insightful. Having personally learned from her for four years, I can see how these experiences from her time as a student really shaped her style as a professor and historian.

"Having trusted advisors opened the doors to a lot of possibilities. There were opportunities for collaboration and discussion. Once I had my PhD, I spent three years as a postdoctoral research associate; I got that post because of my advisors. They already have reputations in the field, and so having studied with them said something about me." What I really loved was how Jill and her advisors' relationship evolved over time. When she was no longer their student and suddenly their colleague, she realized the standards they held her to, which she met, indicated to them that she was their equal once having completed her work. "If I ever needed advice about publishing or looking for jobs, the first people I would go to are Campbell and Dempsey. They are my colleagues now but will always be mentors as well." That role of mentorship is important and unique in many ways. It allows you to learn from, create with, and open doors for one another, all of which can be very collaborative.

Jill also touched on how some of her female mentors really shaped the way she saw herself and her place in the field. "It was really important for me as a young scholar emerging from graduate school to see women at the top of the field working and doing research." In a field that was dominated by men for so long, it really encouraged Jill to see she could have a place in it alongside other esteemed women. Among those female mentors were Elizabeth Cropper, Theresa O'Malley, and Helen Tangires. "I found these women in high-level positions with lots of published works and I was able to observe that. It was really important for young women emerging from school to have models of what is possible. You can look at them and see that it could be possible for you. A lot of my role models didn't have females to look up to when they were taking on the field, so they had to set the stage." And set the stage they did: Jill was able to adopt and absorb so much from her mentors, which in turn she passed along to her students, including myself. This type of collaboration is not outright, but it is so powerful. Students learn so much from their instructors that they can adapt into ways that work for them.

I am extremely grateful for the educators who have encouraged me since I was young and through my college career. When I began interviewing Jill, our conversation turned toward how mentorship made a difference in her career, and a fascinating concept occurred to me: there is this inherent collaboration in mentorship that I had never considered until now.

The advisors that guided Jill were inspired and shaped by their advisors, just as Jill was shaped by them, and I was shaped by Jill. It is important to remember that every mentor you have was once a mentee, and every mentee you may have has the opportunity to grow into a mentor. In the same way, Leonardo da Vinci was once a student; he eventually became a master. This tradition of mentorship is a crucial part of emerging into our own renaissance.

I remember the first day of classes my freshman year of college—I called my mom after Jill's art history class and told her how impressed I was. I have always admired how articulate and intelligent Jill is when she speaks, and I aspired to be as eloquent as her someday. After four years of guidance, advice, and gentle nudges in the right direction, I realize I would not have been capable of completing this book without Jill as my mentor. All the meticulous *Chicago Manual of Style* citations (that I hated) are the same format I needed for this book. The high standards that I was held to for all of my work have made me able to expect it of myself with this project. My work on my thesis and the process I went through with Jill of writing, editing, revising, and finalizing was preparing me for *this*. I mentioned earlier that we are the sum of our parts, and the most significant part of my academic career has been shaped by and modeled after Jill. So in the way that life always seems to, things have come full circle. As I begin to see this age as the beginning of a Neo-Renaissance, I can only hope that I am Jill's Leonardo.

APPENDIX

INTRODUCTION
"These Age Groups Most Affected by COVID-Related Depression, Anxiety."
Hartford HealthCare. Accessed October 11, 2020.
https://hartfordhealthcare.org/about-us/news-press/news-detail?articleid=26831.

Welch, Sydney. "An Analysis of the Attribution of the Louvre Abu Dhabi *Salvator
Mundi*." Undergraduate thesis, Arcadia University, 2020. n.p.

THE SALVATOR MUNDI
Welch, Sydney. "An Analysis of the Attribution of the Louvre Abu Dhabi *Salvator
Mundi*." Undergraduate thesis, Arcadia University, 2020. n.p.

LEONARDO DA VINCI AND THE ITALIAN RENAISSANCE WORKSHOP
"Did Coca-Cola Create Santa Claus?: The Coca-Cola Company." The Coca-Cola
Company: Refresh the World. Make a Difference. Accessed October 11, 2020.
https://www.coca-colacompany.com/faqs/did-coca-cola-invent-santa.

Jeffries, David. "Lil Dicky: Biography & History." AllMusic. Accessed October 11, 2020.
https://www.allmusic.com/artist/lil-dicky-mn0003400565/biography.

Kanter, Laurence. *Leonardo: Discoveries from Verrochio's Studio: Early Paintings and
New Attributions*. New Haven, CT: Yale University Press, 2018.

Syson, Luke. "Leonardo and Leonardism in Renaissance Milan," in *Artists at Court,*
ed. Stephen J. Campbell., 106–23. Boston, Isabella Stewart Gardner Museum, 2004.

Welch, Sydney. "An Analysis of the Attribution of the Louvre Abu Dhabi
Salvator Mundi." Undergraduate thesis, Arcadia University, 2020. n.p.

THE MODERN WORKSHOP TRADITION WITH BOBBY CLOUGHEN
Kerns, Ed. "About." Ed Kerns. Accessed October 11, 2020.
https://edkernsart.com/about-1.

THE SCIENCE OF COLLABORATION
"Collaboration." Merriam-Webster. Merriam-Webster. Accessed October 11, 2020.
https://www.merriam-webster.com/dictionary/collaboration.

Suval, Lauren. "What Drives Our Need For Approval?" World of Psychology, July 8, 2018.
https://psychcentral.com/blog/what-drives-our-need-for-approval/.

Tupula, Gabriel. "Council Post: Position Over Title: Increasing Collaboration In The
Workplace." Forbes. Forbes Magazine, June 19, 2020.
https://www.forbes.com/sites/forbesbusinesscouncil/2020/06/22/position-over-title-
increasing-collaboration-in-the-workplace/.

Vardhman, Raj, Aleksandar Dimovski, and Mateja Velimirovic. "24+ Mesmerizing
Workplace Collaboration Statistics for 2020." goremotely, September 9, 2020.
https://goremotely.net/blog/workplace-collaboration/.

MIXING IT UP WITH REMIX FITNESS
Wadyka, Sally. "7 Reasons to Switch Up Your Workout." One Medical, December 7, 2018.
https://www.onemedical.com/blog/live-well/7-reasons-to-switch-up-your-workout.

VERSATILITY AND ADAPTABILITY WITH THE
HOMESTEAD AND KYLE SCHACHNER
Horne, Katie. "Scary (But True) Small Business Statistics You Can't Afford To
Ignore." Digital.com. Digital.com, August 25, 2020.
https://digital.com/small-business-statistics/.

COLLABORATION OVER COMPETITION WITH
FORMAL FITNESS TRAINING
"The Secret To Success: Don't Compete ... Dominate." Business Trends and Insights.
Accessed October 10, 2020.
https://www.americanexpress.com/en-us/business/trends-and-insights/articles/the-
secret-to-success-dont-compete-dominate/.

CPSIA information can be obtained
at www.ICGtesting.com
Printed in the USA
BVHW091612211220
596052BV00007B/14